My Pen Pal Scrapbook

An educational journey through world cultures

Written and illustrated by Shelley Aliotti

World View Publishers

Tiburon, California

First printing: July 1995   10 9 8 7 6 5 4 3 2

Library of Congress Catalog No.: 95-61366

ISBN: 0-9647396-0-7

MGDigital Atlas is a trademark of Magellan™ Geographix.

Printed by Shepard Poorman, Indianapolis, Indiana
Color reproduction by Metagraphics, Palo Alto, California

Printed in the United States of America on recycled paper

This book is dedicated to dreams and dreamers…

To my mother Ginny, who has taught me to soar and go after my dreams.
To my husband John, for his unconditional love and steadfast support.
To Ben and Laurie, for extending their hands and their hearts to make this dream come true.
To my sons, Jason and Gianni, who have yet to realize all their dreams, but I know they will.

Written and illustrated by Shelley Aliotti
Edited by Diane Tapscott
Designed by Cheryl Moreno

The Pen Pal Kids and their families:

Gianni Aliotti, Nicole Aliotti; Abrahim Al-Marashi, Huda and Laila Al-Marashi; Karri Atherton;
Tara Benkner; Kris Bonifas, Josh Bonifas; Christopher Brant and Thomas and Alexander Brant;
Enole Ede and Jonathon, Kelly, Rosalind, Okopi, and Godwin Ede; Rosamarie Guttierez; Jim Hsu;
Deandra Lee; Skip Lind; Laura Moreno; Seema Patel and Amirash, Dharti, Pragna, and Sapna Patel;
Elina Raskin; Jason Reisig-Aliotti; Jennifer Rosenthal, Danny Rosenthal; Carolyn Smith;
Ellis Smith; Tessa Tapscott; Thalia Tardivet; Chad Trainer; and Giuseppina Ventimiglia

*For carefully reviewing the letters and for generously sharing their keepsakes,
mementos, and photos we thank:*

Niniv Abrahim, Cass and Marian Aliotti, Sabah Al-Marashi, Rita Amladi, Ben Askarinam,
Elizabeth Bertrand, John and Sandy Bonifas, Anna Brady, Ingrid Brant, the Roger Consani family,
the Dean Diaz family, Andre and Laurie Francot, Brad Gorman, Michael M. Gray, Gloria Hughes,
Rachel Joseph, Robert Krohn, Nina Laub, Tanya Melnick, Andre Muller, Pragna Patel,
Elizabeth Phillips, Melissa Pickford, Richard and Kate Rosenthal, Evan Smith, Ginny Smith,
Yoshie Wirks, Maria Vargas, Min Wang, Tanya Wendling, and Lucy Zaracua

Special thanks to:

The Saudi Arabian Oil Company, the Monterey Museum of Art, the Saudi Arabian Embassy,
the Indian Embassy, and the 5th grade students from Carmel Mission and River Elementary schools
in Carmel, and from Tularicitos Elementary School in Carmel Valley

Back cover photo by Aamon Kennedy
Copyedited by Pat Soberanis
Country maps created using MGDigital Atlas™ software
and customized by Rachel Stevens

USA

Dear Pen Pal,

Hello, my name is Jessica. I am from the United States of America, and this is how it all began. Summer vacation was almost over and most of my friends were out of town. I didn't know what to do. If I told Mom I was bored, she would immediately list a thousand things that I could do, like clean my closet, sweep the deck, or do something totally honorable like collecting old clothes from the neighbors to give to a charity. Knowing the danger, I braced myself and said, "Mom, I'm bored!"

I was only half-listening when I heard her mention something that really did interest me: " . . . or you could write a letter to a pen pal from another country . . . " A pen pal? Hey, that sounded like a good idea! I enjoy writing and I love to travel and learn about new places. Mom was thrilled. Then she told me about Samantha Smith. Samantha was a young schoolgirl from Maine. Sometime in the early 1980s she was very concerned about the possibility of war with the Soviet Union. So she decided to write a letter to Mr. Andropov, who was the president of the Soviet Union! She told him how much she really wanted peace in the world and asked him if he really wanted to start a war. He wrote back to her saying no, he didn't want war, he wanted peace too. He invited Samantha and her parents to visit him in the Soviet Union and meet some Russian families, so they did! Isn't that a great story? That's when I realized that kids, just like us, really can make a difference in the world!

My parents have always made me feel that what I think matters. They encourage me to express my feelings, and we talk about whatever worries me. I told Mom that like Samantha, I'm also afraid of war and want peace in the world. I asked her if she thought there could ever be world peace. She said, "Until people, wherever they live, have peace within themselves, it will be impossible for there to be world peace. Peace starts inside each of us. It is expressed in the way we live our lives and by our actions. That's why I practice meditation. It helps me feel peaceful inside and toward others."

When I went to bed that night, I couldn't stop thinking about Samantha and about what Mom said about peace. Mom meditates every morning. What could I do to feel more peaceful? The next day, I took a long walk on the beach, and wondered about how I could help make the world a peaceful place. How could I make a difference, even if people aren't always peaceful? Then I thought about kids in other

countries and wondered how they live. What do they like to do and what are their families like? What are their countries like? Does their religion give them a feeling of peace? Do they want a peaceful world too? I wondered if they thought kids could make a difference. I went home to get started.

Mom had gotten me some names and addresses of pen pals from different countries around the world. I picked out 16 names from 16 countries, and now I'm writing to you on my new Macintosh computer— it's really fun! I want to learn about you and how you live. For example, I have a collection of angels that I bought in different places we've been to. I believe each of us has an angel who watches over us. Do you? Are there angels in your culture? Please write and tell me all about yourself. I want to learn about you and, if you want, you can learn about me. I'm going to make a scrapbook of all the letters and photos I receive, or any other stuff you send me. I also love to draw and have started drawing pictures about all the countries I am writing to from books I got at the library.

So now I'll tell you about me. I live in the town of Carmel in California. California has more people than any other state in the United States of America. It's on the West Coast. I have a younger brother, Jason, and a younger sister named Alexandra, but we call her Lexi. She's only three and a half. Jason's pretty good for a brother and only a pest when my friends are over. He's the catcher on his Little League baseball team. He's a good player and loves baseball. So does my dad, who coaches the team. He also plays golf. That's not what he does for work, though. My dad is a contractor. He builds houses and other buildings. My mom is a travel agent. She helps people plan trips. Maybe that's what I'll be, because I love to travel. Or maybe I'll be a veterinarian or a journalist. I don't know yet.

I love to draw, like I said, but I also love animals, music, reading books, and going to the movies. I even like school. We have a yellow Labrador retriever named Jake and a cat named Syd. They are both part of our family. We also have deer living in the meadow behind our house, and gray squirrels with bushy tails that chase each other around the tall pine trees. There are raccoons that come out at night, and Monarch butterflies that come back to this area every fall for the winter. I wonder where they come back from?

Since our house is just a few blocks from the Pacific Ocean, we go to the beach a lot. We may take a picnic, play volleyball on the sand, or just take a walk. Sometimes we climb on the rocks and explore the tide pools. I think I'm most

peaceful when I'm at the beach. I like watching the pelicans swoop down for fish, and you can see seals and sea otters playing in the waves. At the Monterey Bay Aquarium in Monterey, which is the city next to Carmel, they have many of the creatures that live in our bay in giant tanks and pools. You can pet a bat ray and see sea otters "up close and personal." They're so cute and smart. When a sea otter eats, it lies on its back with a rock on its stomach, and it uses the rock to crack shellfish. I'm glad that Monterey Bay was just made a "marine sanctuary," which means it will always be protected, just like a national park.

Our family also likes to go to the shopping mall. Shopping malls have everything: restaurants (I love Mexican and Italian food!), movie theaters, video arcades, department stores, and every kind of shop you could want. Sometimes they have craft fairs, or artists who perform right there! Some malls even have carousels, and the mall near my cousin's house has an ice-skating rink.

When I tell someone I'm from California, they always think I live near Disneyland or Hollywood, but I don't. Those places are in southern California, about seven hours away by car. I live about three hours south of San Francisco. If you visited me, we would take you there. It's a beautiful city, with lots of great things to see. Where would you take me if I visited you?

On vacations my family loves to travel. Last summer we drove our minivan all the way across the country to the East Coast. Now I understand how huge my country is! My dad said you can take the interstate highway and travel from coast to coast, almost 3,000 miles, without ever seeing a stoplight! But we stopped all along the way. By the time we got to the Grand Canyon in Arizona, we had seen license plates from every state in the nation. The Grand Canyon is the most unbelievable natural wonder I've ever seen! It's awesome! They say it was once under water. When you look down into the canyon from the top, the Colorado River looks like a thin ribbon winding along the bottom. We took a donkey ride down into the canyon. Lexi cried at first and I don't blame her; it was a little scary!

We left the canyon and drove through the desert and saw cactus and red-clay bluffs under the brightest of blue skies! My favorite stop was exploring the cliff dwellings of the Anasazi Indians. Visiting the tribal sites and museums there gave me a picture of the way they lived. It seemed to me they lived close to the earth

and were in touch with nature. I wonder if that made them feel peaceful? We also visited the pueblo homes of the Native Americans that live in New Mexico near Santa Fe and Taos. I enjoyed seeing their jewelry, weaving, and pottery. My parents bought me a clay storyteller doll from the Cochiti Pueblo. Each pueblo has their own style of pottery as well as their own stories to tell. Since our trip I have been fascinated with Native Americans, our country's first inhabitants. There were Native Americans living on the Monterey Peninsula long before California was made a Spanish colony. They were peaceful fishermen. They helped Father Junipero Serra, an early missionary, build the Carmel Mission over 200 years ago. Some Sundays we go to mass there, and sometimes we go to the Presbyterian Church, where my grandmother sings in the choir. To me, they're just different places and ways to worship the same God.

Back to our trip. We also visited Washington, D.C., our nation's capital. I especially liked the Lincoln Memorial. The statue of Abraham Lincoln inside the building is gigantic. It really makes Lincoln seem larger than life. We also took a tour of the White House, where the president and his family lives. From Washington, we went to New York City. It's our largest city. There are tall skyscrapers, like the World Trade Center and the Empire State Building, and lots of apartment houses. The streets are crowded with people hurrying around, and incredible stores, restaurants, art galleries, and museums. We took a ferry boat to see the Statue of Liberty. You can go up in an elevator and walk around in her face and crown. What a view!

When I went back to school, I wrote about the trip. I titled my paper "What Is America?" because America has so many faces. There are small towns and big cities. In some places there are farms and cornfields as far as you can see. We also have deserts, palm trees, and beaches, and forests and snowcapped mountains too. There are small towns where every house has a front porch for visiting with your neighbors, and cities where no one seems to know each other. But what America is, I think, is all these things and all the different people. That's what makes my country so interesting.

My ancestry is English and French on my mother's side and Italian on my father's. That makes me a "mix," and that too is typically American. The United States is a huge country made up of people from many different nationalities, religions, and

5

cultures, like a big melting pot. I ended my school paper with the words that are written on the statue of "Miss Liberty," which has been standing in New York Harbor for over 100 years: "Give me your tired, your poor, your huddled masses yearning to be free . . . " She represents the many different nationalities of people who have come to America, all so different and yet so similar at the same time! Everyone who comes to live here is looking for a better life. My teacher said he thinks of America more as a pot of stew than a melting pot. The flavors of the ingredients taste good together but each ingredient is still distinct. In our country, different ethnic groups melt together to make one United States of America, but each group keeps their own customs and has their own flavor, just like the stew. I like that. I think that is the beauty of America.

Now I'd like to learn more about you, your country, and how you live. Do you think we can make a difference in the world? Maybe we can be teachers for each other. Maybe by finding out about each other we will discover that even though we have differences, we really are very much the same. What if Mom is right and peace does start within each of us? What if peace is like a pebble thrown into water? It makes ripples, and those ripples circle out into bigger and bigger circles until the whole world is a peaceful and loving place. Then we should do whatever we can in our own part of the world to encourage love and peace among the people around us. We could think of ourselves as a Junior Peace Force. Do you share my thoughts? What do you think? Please write back soon, I can't wait to hear from you!

Your Pen Pal,

Jessica

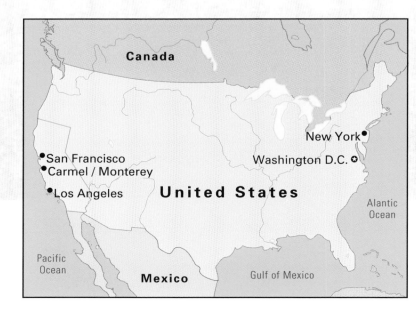

Dear Pen Pal,

Konichiwa. Hello. My name is Michiko. My friends call me Michi. I like very much your idea to write to kids all over the world! I never heard the story about Samantha Smith before. Her letter to the Russian president did make a difference! I would love to be your Japanese pen pal and be part of your Junior Peace Force!

I like to write letters, but in school writing is my most difficult subject. You are lucky, you only have 26 letters in your alphabet. In Japanese, there are three alphabets—Kata Kana, Kanji, and Romaji. I believe there are millions of characters to learn to write in Japanese. My teacher says I exaggerate, as always. There are only thousands! I also like school, like you. It is a good thing because we go to school until 5:00 in the evening and half a day on Saturdays. It is very important to me to do well in school, so I work hard at my lessons.

I like very much the watercolor painting class I am taking. It is very difficult to control the paint. If you do not, you have a very big mess. I am most proud of my painting of a cherry tree. Every spring we celebrate the beauty of these trees at the Cherry Blossom Festival.

Everyone in Japan loves to fly kites, not just children, but adults too! Our ancestors believed that flying a kite over your roof kept away evil spirits. The Japanese think kites are magical and that, through the wind, they connect us to the heavens. In Japan, kites come in all sizes, colors, and shapes. Dragon designs ("tatsu") are very popular. Do you fly kites at the beach in Carmel?

I am sending you the Kanji characters that we use to spell the name of my country, Nihon (Japan). Nihon means "land of the rising sun." Japan is a string of islands in the Pacific Ocean near Asia. The four main islands are Hokkaido, Honshu, Shikoku, and Kyushu, and there are hundreds of smaller ones. My family lives in the city of Kawasaki, near Tokyo, on the island of Honshu. Most Japanese

people live in cities along the coasts. We are a very crowded country, since it is about the size of California with more than half the population of the entire United States!

Last month, we took a trip to visit our cousins, Yoshie and Kaoru, in Kyoto. We went on the Bullet Train (we call it the Shinkansen). It was the fastest train in the world, but now there is a train in France they say is faster. If the weather is clear we can see Fuji-san out the window. We think Mount Fuji is very beautiful and it is a symbol for our country. It is the tallest mountain in Japan, and it is also a volcano. We have many earthquakes here. I know you have earthquakes in California too. I do not like earthquakes. The people of Kobe, the epicenter of the big earthquake of 1995, are still rebuilding their homes and city. Luckily, the famous temples of the ancient capital, Kyoto, were not badly harmed.

You wrote that your brother plays on a baseball team. "Yakyuu," or baseball, is also very popular in Japan. We sometimes go to a baseball game at Korakuen Stadium. My brother says he will be a baseball star when he grows up. I told him he needs a lot more practice. My father loves to play golf. He said that maybe someday we will come to visit you. Then he can play golf at the famous courses near you! When my father has vacation time, we like to travel. He works for a company that makes electronic products. Perhaps you have video games, a television, or a stereo that my fathers' company made.

Japan is an island, so fishing is a big business here. We eat fish and gohan (rice), almost every day. Gohan means "meal," so without rice, there is no meal. Sometimes I like going to restaurants where I can eat American foods, like hamburgers, french fries, and ice cream, but my favorite food is sushi. I help my mother prepare it. We roll raw fish, vegetables, and rice in seaweed. I like to dip sushi in wasabi (a hot green paste) and soy sauce. Whenever we prepare food, we pay careful attention to make it as pleasing to the eye as to the taste!

Sometimes my parents drink tiny cups of hot rice wine called sake, but we usually all drink green tea. Do you drink tea? If you came to visit us, Mama-san would honor you as her guest at a traditional tea ceremony. Tea ceremony is performed very precisely. It teaches us to appreciate simple things and to notice small details. Maybe it is like the meditation you say your mother does. My mother says the tea ceremony makes her feel very peaceful and calm. I think it also teaches patience, because you have to kneel for so long! Normally, I wear clothes like yours, but tea ceremony is a special occasion. For this I wear my silk kimono. It was my great-grandmother's. On the 3rd of March, we celebrate Girl's Day. This is also called the Festival of the Dolls. I sent you a kokeshi doll. It is a very typical doll in Japan. On Girl's Day, we display dolls called "hinaningyoo" wearing traditional kimonos. All young girls wear their best kimonos and visit their friends. Just like there is a special way to perform tea ceremony, there is also a special way to wear a kimono. All kimonos are basically the same shape; it is how you tie the "obi," which is like a sash or belt, that makes the difference. My mother says, "To make the kimono beautiful, we must first make our inner self, our spirit, a thing of beauty, because the kimono shows, not hides, your inner qualities." There is also a Boy's Day Festival on May 5. On that day, families with boys hang "koinobori," or carp streamers, outside. The streamers look like carp swimming vigorously in the water and remind boys to have a positive spirit.

We have many customs I could teach you about. We never wear our shoes in the house. We always take them off before we enter and put on a pair of slippers. We keep extra pairs of slippers for our guests. We always bow when we greet someone, a small bow for family or friends, a deeper one for older people, and a much deeper bow when we are visiting a temple or shrine.

I also enjoy going to the movies. But if you were to visit me, my parents might take you to see the Kabuki theater. In Kabuki, the actors paint their faces to represent their characters. The "oyama," or female parts, are played by men with lots of makeup. Kabuki theater is very spectacular. The stage has parts that revolve, and I love the elaborate costumes the Kabuki actors wear. At Kabuki you can learn about our customs and traditions as our history is acted out in dramatic living pictures. Grandfather says that it is very important for us to remember our history and culture.

November 15 is Shichi-go-san, Children's Day. During this festival, children dress in their best clothes and visit the temples and shrines. I enjoy spending extra time in the gardens outside. Some gardens have miniature lakes with tiny islands and bridges. These peaceful gardens always bring me happiness. My family is Buddhist. I have read stories about Buddha. Sometimes he would sit in the garden to meditate and find answers to questions he might have. Meditation is one of the three teachings that Buddha wrote about. The other two are ethics, or how we behave, and wisdom. He taught that to become wise and have happiness, we first must have a calm and strong mind to help us choose between good and bad.

When I need answers, I find a quiet place to think. Then, when my mind is quiet, I see things more clearly. The mind is like a glass of saltwater. If you shake it up, it is cloudy and you cannot see. When the water is still, the salt goes to the bottom and the water becomes clear. To clear his mind, my father spends hours in his garden caring for his tiny bonsai trees. After commuting on a crowded subway and working in a crowded office, he likes to come home to his "little island of peace."

Buddhism teaches me to practice compassion, love, and kindness. I think most religions share this teaching. This might sound simple, but sometimes it is hard to practice. Being angry or hateful to others will not give us inner peace, but having a good feeling toward others will. I think that global peace begins with inner peace. I think that if we try to understand the different ways people live and think, then we can learn to respect each other and have world peace.

Sayonara,

Michi

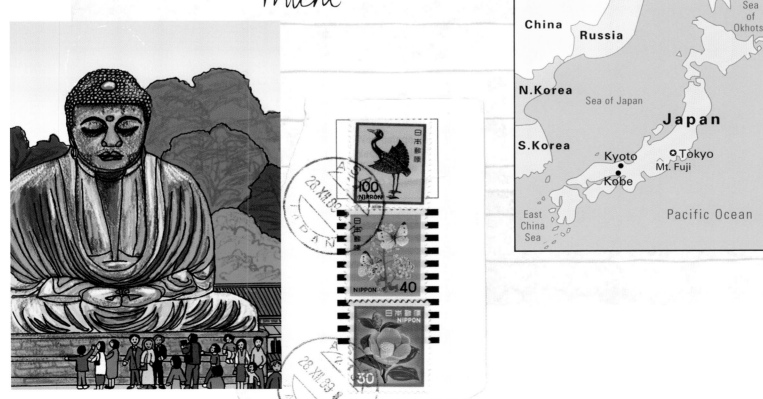

australia

Dear Pen Pal,

G'day! My name is Peter and I'm from Australia. Australia means "southland," but because it is below the equator we call it Down Under. And because we are on the other side of the equator, our seasons are just the opposite of yours. When it's summer for you, we're having winter! When you're skiing and making snowmen, we're probably wearing shorts and cooking our dinner on the "barbie" (that's a barbeque, not a doll!). Even though we speak the same language, I think many of the meanings for the same words are different.

In my family there is me, my folks, and my four brothers—Robert, Christopher, Alex, and Thomas. We live on a sheep station near Sydney. You could say that sheep raising is in our blood. My great-great-grandfather was a farmer in Great Britain. He heard that the grazing land here was good, so he decided to move to Australia and raise wool to ship around the world. Supposedly a lot of criminals were sent here from England, but some people moved here looking for gold, like during the gold rush in California. If they didn't find any gold, some must have decided to become sheep ranchers, because there are more sheep here than people now. Australia has become the greatest wool-producing country in the world, fair dinkum. (That means "It's true, mate!")

You'd really enjoy watching our "kelpies" (sheepdogs). They herd the sheep by barking at them and nipping at their ankles. They keep the sheep where they're supposed to be, or move them where they need to go. Kelpies are born to herd, but they still need a little training. If only we could teach them to shear sheep (give them "haircuts")! I call my favorite dog Bluey. At night, she always sleeps on the rug next to my bed.

Sydney is the capital of New South Wales, one of Australia's six states (there are also two territories). Sydney is very modern, with a beautiful and busy seaport. A huge bridge crosses over Botany Bay from Sydney to North Shore, or you can take a ferry boat. Have you ever seen a picture of Sydney's Opera House? It's very famous. Some people think it looks like a pile of seashells. I think it looks like sailboats racing in the harbor.

Australia's the largest island and the smallest continent in the whole world. In fact, it is the only country that fills a whole continent. And because it is so isolated, it's sort of a "natural zoo." There are animals here that aren't found anywhere else! Some are quite strange, yeah. Like the platypus. It has fur like a dog and a bill like a duck. It swims underwater, but lays eggs in a nest. We have lots of interesting

birds too. The emu is similar to an ostrich, and there are penguins that come to the most southern parts of Australia to have their babies. Did you know that penguins and emus can't even fly? Our national bird, the kookaburra, doesn't sing. Instead, it makes a laughing call. You should hear me and my friends try to mimic them. We sound more like a bunch of laughing hyenas!

When you think of Australia, the animals you think of first are probably kangaroos and koala bears. Koalas aren't really bears at all. They're marsupials. So are kangaroos. Marsupial mothers are the only animals that carry their babies in built-in pouches. Koalas live in gum trees (you call them eucalyptus trees) and eat the leaves around them. I would take you to the West Hills Koala Park near Sydney, where the koalas are so tame you could hold them. Kangaroos and wallabies are just about everywhere in Australia, maybe like the deer that live in the meadow near you. Baby kangaroos are called "joeys," and when they are fully grown, they can jump 2 meters high. I wish I could jump that high (so does my sports teacher).

Last January, we spent our summer holiday at the Great Barrier Reef up north, off the coast of Queensland. It's a coral reef that's made from the skeletons of tiny animals called coral polyps. Coral polyps are actually little animals that live in the reef along with millions of colorful fish. We snorkeled in the reef every day. The fish are so funny, they come right up to you. I saw green turtles, giant clams, jellyfish, eels, and dolphins. My brother Robert is a photographer and takes pictures when he dives. I sent you one showing a fish underneath a piece of coral. Isn't it interesting? I also sent you a turtle souvenir. We watched turtles being born! You just sit quietly on the beach, and all of a sudden they burst out of the sand and go running all about. Australia has lots of long, sandy beaches, with huge waves that are perfect for surfing. My brother Christopher is a great surfer. He meets surfers from all over the world, and many are from California. He wants to go to California someday to surf. Maybe he'll take me with him and I can visit you!

The western part of Australia is mostly desert. My friend Andy lives near a place called Alice Springs in the Northern Territory. We call this area the "outback" or the "bush." The summers there are much too hot and dry for me, but Andy seems to like it. In fact, it's so hot that the rivers dry up, and then the people have "dry" boat races. You should see it! They dress up like boats and race along the dry riverbeds. The outback is very interesting, but it can be lonely too. Towns might be 300 or 400 kilometers apart! I think Andy gets a little lonely. I know I would. He doesn't go to a regular school like I do. He gets his paper and pencils and books, and then turns on the radio! Andy studies on a two-way radio with a teacher from

the School of the Air. He has to send in his homework by mail! And if you need a doctor in the outback, they make house calls by plane. It's called the Royal Flying Doctor Service.

I guess Andy and I are pen pals too, but we visit each other a couple of times a year. The last time I saw Andy in the outback, we went to the Kakadu National Park and stayed in the Gagaduju Crocodile Hotel. It's designed to look like a croc-odile! Did you ever see the movie *Crocodile Dundee?* This is where it takes place, in the outback. On the same trip we went to Ayer's Rock, nicknamed the "largest pebble in the world." It's a monolith, one huge rock the size of a mountain. It sits alone in the middle of the flatland and changes color, depending on what time of day it is and how the light hits it. At sunset it can glow pink, or orange, or red, fair dinkum. The Aborigines call it Uluru and think it's sacred.

Aborigine means "first inhabitant." They have been in Australia for 40,000 years. European settlers have only been here for 200 years. Like your Native Americans, the Aborigines are Australia's original people and one of the world's oldest cultures. Many Aborigines have become stockmen or cowboys on the cattle stations, or work at regular jobs, so they no longer live on the land the way they used to. On weekends, though, many take their children to experience life exactly as their fore-fathers did thousands of years ago. They gather, hunt, and fish, and live outside. They do this so their children don't forget where they came from. Some people say the Aborigines have the best eyesight of anybody. And they make some of their own tools by hand, like the boomerang. You must have heard of the boomerang. It was originally used to stun an animal so they could catch or kill it for food.

From spending time with Andy in the outback, I have become very interested in the Aborigines and their culture. I did a report on them for school. I learned that the Aborigines believe in harmony in nature and that we should care for all forms of life. They live close to the earth and think that there are spirits, sort of like angels, everywhere—in trees, rivers, rocks, and in animals too. They memorize hundreds of songs, dances, and stories that they share in festive ceremonies. This is how their history is passed to their children. They are the great storytellers of our land. I spent some time with an old Aborigine who's lived in the outback all his life. His story about the Wandjinas fascinated me. Wandjinas are mythical sky heroes who made the land at the time of dreaming. (The "time of dreaming" is when the Aborigines believe the world was created.) He told me he "invites" dreaming to come to him. He says he can dream the future and gets clues for understanding the past. I told him that I have colorful dreams with lots of detail.

He said I should remember my dreams and learn to use them to help solve every-day problems. Do you think that really works? Do you have dreams?

The most important thing I think we can learn from the ancient wisdom of the Aborigine culture is to stop abusing the earth before it's too late! To them, the earth is more than a thing of beauty that provides for us. To Aborigines, the earth is divine. They call it Kunapipi, the Great Mother. They think man has misused the land by destroying the ozone layer, creating environmental pollution, and using the earth's natural resources carelessly. They think we should pass the earth to our children in the same condition, or even better, than it came to us. I think if we take the best things from the Old World, and the best of the New World, we can make the earth a better place to live.

You know what a boomerang is. If you throw it, it's supposed to come back to you. It takes a lot of practice to learn to throw a boomerang. We also use the word "boomerang" to mean something you expect to get back. Say I loan you some money, or my jacket. It's as if I'm giving you a boomerang that I want to come back. My father says that life can be a boomerang too. What we give out, whether we are honest or dishonest, kind or cruel, loving or hateful, will come right back to us, just like a boomerang!

Well, mate, "ooroo," or see you later. Remember, this letter is a boomerang, so I hope you send one back to me!

Your Mate from Down Under,

Peter

italy

Dear Pen Pal,

Ciao! Hello! My name is Gianni. I come from a country in the Mediterranean Sea. It is the shape of a boot and looks like it is kicking the island of Sicily like a soccer ball. Do you recognize it? It is Italia, or Italy for you. I live where the "knee" is, just outside the city of Firenze, or, as you would say in English, Florence.

Toscana (Tuscany) is the area of Italy where you will find Firenze. It looks exactly like the landscapes that the Italian masters have been painting for hundreds of years. There are rolling hills covered with grapevines, umbrella pines, and chestnut and olive trees, and there are sheep sprinkled on the hillsides. Past the hills, tiled roofs cast a rusty glow over the city of Florence. It is "bellissimo," very beautiful! Mama says I have the eye of an artist and the pen of a poet! But Papa, he hopes I will follow in the family business because I am the oldest child. For five generations my family has grown and pressed olives for cooking oil. We also grow grapes for the Chianti wine that Tuscany is known for. But I think I always have been, and always will be, an artist. I will not spend my life at the "frantoio" (olive press)!

I have heard people say that in Italy, people cook with passion. In Tuscany, cooking is an art. Tuscan cooks use the same basic ingredients their Etruscan ancestors did: bread, wine, and olive oil. I guess everyone thinks their mother is the best cook. I know I do! Mama's food is "magnifico"! Her grilled meats, soups, and stews are delicious, but her homemade ravioli are "buonissimi"! She says all you need to make great pasta is flour and eggs, two hands, and a big heart! Nonna (my grandmother) says that being Italian is like a feeling. A feeling of fun and hospitality, a sharing with friends or strangers who happen to come by at dinnertime. She is always telling everyone to "mangiamo, mangia!" which means, "eat, eat!" My grandfather, Nonno, he says Italians are passionate people who are always quick to return a smile. I know my family loves to laugh and wave our hands around when we talk. I do not think we could communicate without using our hands! To me, the word that describes us is "entusiasmo" (enthusiastic). Mama says that enthusiasm is a great gift. But to keep it, you must also give it away! She also tells me that if I do what I love to do, like my art or music, or playing soccer, I will succeed and be happy. And my mama, she is always right!

My family works very hard during the week. I go to school every day from 8:00 a.m. to 12:30 p.m., Monday through Saturday. Then I come home to do my homework and chores. Tomorrow is Sunday, our special day of rest. It is a day to play and be with family. After church we sometimes go to the piazza. The piazza is a perfect place to watch people, which I love to do. People are funny or serious, tall or short, fat or thin. It is very interesting to see how different we can be! I sit in the piazza eating gelato and I just watch. The best gelato is "bacio," which means kiss. It is creamy chocolate gelato with crunchy nuts. But no matter what we do during the day, Sunday dinner is always spent with my family and grandparents.

Papa and Nonno love to play cards and bocce bol, a bowling game. I enjoy playing with them, but soccer is my favorite sport. My brother Carlo and I play on a soccer team. My sisters, Marianna and Francesca, play volleyball. There is also much interest here in bicycle and auto racing. Italians make some of the finest cars in the world. Ferraris, Alfa Romeos, and Lamborghinis, they are all made in Italy! But I could probably say that Italians are soccer crazy! We might not all play, but we all watch! And you can be sure that whatever the sport is, the crowds in our stadiums will be full of entusiasmo!

On special holidays my family drives to Florence and we go to the Duomo. That is the big cathedral there. We also walk along the Ponte Vecchio, which is the oldest bridge in the city. My sisters like to go there because it is full of jewelry stores. But my favorite place to visit in Florence is the Uffizi gallery because it has one of the most magnifico art collections in the world. That is where I got this postcard of Raphael's "putto" for your angel collection. Putto are guardian angels who protect us all through our lives. I believe we each have one. I think you believe that also, yes? Florence was an art center during the Renaissance. That was the greatest of all art ages. Michelangelo and Leonardo da Vinci were born here. I have seen almost all of Michelangelo's paintings and sculptures. His sculpture, *David,* is so wonderful. The marble that *David* is carved from actually seems to glow! Someday, I will go to Milan to see da Vinci's painting, *The Last Supper,* and to Paris to see his most famous portrait, *Mona Lisa*.

Last summer, my Uncle Tony, who is also an artist, took me to Rome. He knew how much I wanted to see Michelangelo's famous ceiling in the Sistine Chapel. He had to lay on his back on a scaffold to paint the ceiling. It took him four years to finish it, even with assistants! I would also show you the ancient ruins in Rome. You can almost feel the history around you. When I was at the Forum, I imagined Caesar speaking to his Senate and could practically hear the Roman chariots race around the Piazza Navona.

It seems that you and I both love to travel. I think you would love Venezia, yes? My first trip to Venice was when I was two years old. I still remember sitting in the piazza, surrounded by pigeons because the bag of corn my father had given me to feed them had spilled into my lap. Here is the photo Mama took that day. Pigeons are sitting all over me, on my back, my arms, my head, everywhere! Venice is a very old and beautiful city. It was built on a hundred islands that are connected by footbridges. There are canals instead of streets, so there are no cars or trucks, just boats. There are delivery boats stacked with fruits and vegetables for market, or pickup boats bringing supplies to the shops. To get from place to place, people ride in water taxis or in "vaporetti," which are bigger boats, more like buses. Or we could ride in a gondola. I am sure you have seen these classic old boats that have been used in Venice for hundreds of years. The gondoliers move them silently through the canals with long poles and they always serenade their riders. People should go through life like this, yes? Peaceful, with a song in their hearts.

You wrote that you love music. What kind do you listen to? My whole family loves music, but we all have different tastes. Nonno says, "Give Italians a mandolin, a song, a crowd, and a little vino and they can turn any day into a feast day!" Father loves Italian opera and says Enrico Caruso was the world's greatest tenor. I prefer Luciano Pavarotti, maybe because he sang in the first opera I ever saw. Have you ever been to an opera? Operas are very dramatic plays, with heroes and villains, wonderful costumes, and elaborate scenery, and the actors sing all of their lines. Opera was born in Italy. I do enjoy going to the opera with my parents, but I like what we call "musicaleggera" (pop music) the best.

You asked how I feel about world peace. Sometimes it is hard to have peace in your own family. Do you know what I mean? With two younger brothers and two older sisters, well, we don't always get along because we are all different. That is when Mama reminds us to love each other and that you should "love your neighbor as yourself." Maybe the world would be more peaceful if people listened to those simple words. Also, I think if you feel good about yourself you can understand, and will maybe accept, others who are different than you are. Just invite them for dinner and, like Nonna, tell them to "mangia!" I hope you like the lace handkerchief. It is from Nonna.

Ciao, arrivederci, so long.

Pace! Peace!

Gianni

Dear Pen Pal,

Shalom. Hello. In Israel, we say "shalom" when we greet someone and when we say good-bye. Shalom means "peace" in Hebrew. My name is Sarah Rebekah. Jewish children are given two names when they are born. One is a popular name or has historical meaning. Our other name is given to us in memory of an important relative, in my case, my grandmother Rebekah. My brother, Daniel Benadam, was named for my father's favorite uncle.

My brother had his Bar Mitzvah last month. That is the ceremony boys have at 13 to mark their passage into the adult community. Danny led some prayers at the service and recited from the Torah, our holy book. You might know, it as the first five books of the Old Testament. Danny had built a wooden replica of the Ark of the Covenant, the sacred golden box that held the Ten Commandments given to Moses. It was displayed at the party after the religious ceremony. He was very proud of it! We celebrated with delicious food and dancing. He got so many presents! I am looking forward to my Bat Mitzvah, a similar ceremony for girls. Mine is next year. To prepare for this, every evening and on Sunday mornings I go to school at the "synagogue" (or house of prayer) to study and practice reading from the Torah. Rabbis, the teachers of our religion, Judaism, teach us how to sing or chant the words I'll need to know. My father is a rabbi, so I get extra help at home!

Jerusalem, where I live, is the capital of Israel. It is divided into three sections: the New City (West Jerusalem), the Old City, and East Jerusalem. My family lives in the New City of Jerusalem. There are many new houses, shopping centers, and modern buildings here. It is quite different and separate from Old Jerusalem, the walled city. Within the tall stone walls of the Old City, you walk into the past on ancient paths, passing many historical monuments. There are cobblestone streets much too narrow for cars, so people use donkeys and camels to carry their heavy loads. Small shops called "souks" line many of the crowded streets. They sell everything from food and spices to clothing, carpets, pottery, jewelry, and, of course, souvenirs for the many tourists. Many Arabs live in East Jerusalem, which is mostly residential.

Jerusalem is a very special city. Millions of people come, not just to see our beautiful country and buildings, but to relive the great events that happened here. Jerusalem is considered a holy city for people of three different religions: the Jews, the Christians, and the Muslims. The three-domed Church of the Holy Sepulchre was built over the tomb of Jesus, from where, Christians believe, he rose to heaven. The Muslims also worship their prophet, Muhammad, at the Dome of the Rock. This building is quite beautiful, with magnificent mosaic walls, arches, and a huge golden dome. And for Jews, like us, this has been a special place since the days of Abraham, an important

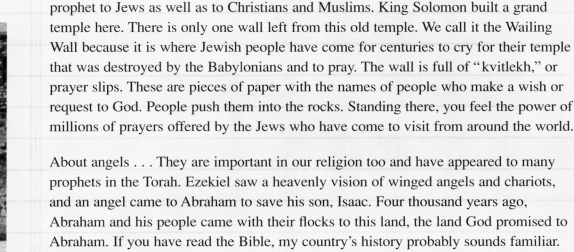

prophet to Jews as well as to Christians and Muslims. King Solomon built a grand temple here. There is only one wall left from this old temple. We call it the Wailing Wall because it is where Jewish people have come for centuries to cry for their temple that was destroyed by the Babylonians and to pray. The wall is full of "kvitlekh," or prayer slips. These are pieces of paper with the names of people who make a wish or request to God. People push them into the rocks. Standing there, you feel the power of millions of prayers offered by the Jews who have come to visit from around the world.

About angels . . . They are important in our religion too and have appeared to many prophets in the Torah. Ezekiel saw a heavenly vision of winged angels and chariots, and an angel came to Abraham to save his son, Isaac. Four thousand years ago, Abraham and his people came with their flocks to this land, the land God promised to Abraham. If you have read the Bible, my country's history probably sounds familiar. These stories, about Abraham and Noah's Ark, are stories you might know from the Old Testament in the Bible and are taught in our schools as our history.

We have many special holidays to celebrate our history. Purim is one of our most festive holidays. Purim honors Esther, the Queen of Persia, because she helped to save the Jews from being massacred by the King's evil advisor Hamam. It also marks the coming of spring, with costumes, carnival processions, and dancing in the streets. Maybe this celebration is a little like your Halloween or Mardi Gras. Rosh ha-Shanah is the celebration of our new year in September. It is not on the same day as yours, because we have a different calendar. On Rosh ha-Shanah a "shofar" is sounded. It's a ram's horn, like the one Moses sounded when he gave the Israelites the Ten Commandments. We sound it now to remind God to open his Book of Life, where all our names are written! Ten days after Rosh ha-Shanah, we have our most holy day, Yom Kippur, when we ask God to forgive our sins.

Sometimes Hanukkah falls at the same time as Christmas. We exchange gifts and have a good time too, but we celebrate Hanukkah for eight days. Each day, we open a present and light a candle on the "menorah," a special candleholder. Pesach, or Passover, is a celebration of our freedom from slavery in Egypt, where Jacob, Abraham's grandson, had led the Jewish people to escape famine. (Jacob had a dream about angels climbing up and down a ladder from Heaven!) On Pesach, we have a banquet called the "seder," and each food we eat has a special meaning. Some foods are sweet, to remember the good times, and some are bitter, so we do not forget the bad times.

For many years our people were ruled by neighboring nations, so many Jews scattered and lived throughout the world because they had no country of their own. But wherever they were, they always prayed and worked toward returning to Jerusalem, to have Passover in their homeland. Yad Vashen, our Holocaust Museum, is a solemn reminder to all its visitors of the millions of Jews who lost their lives just 50 years ago in Nazi concentration camps. Did you visit the Holocaust Museum in Washington,

D.C., on your trip? The concentration camps must never be forgotten, so they can't happen ever again. After World War II, the state of Israel was established as the permanent Jewish homeland. Many Jews, especially from Europe, came to live here, and our people had their own country at last.

At any celebration, I especially love folk dancing to the music and rhythms of the many different countries our people have lived in. The Hora, which is now considered our national dance, actually came from Rumania. It is not danced in couples. Instead, a whole group dances in a big circle. The circle symbolizes unity. The music and dancing starts slow and gradually gets faster and faster and faster! It is so much fun—we sing and laugh! Danny plays the drums and my father has a beautiful voice; he sings at the synagogue. I would say that my whole family is quite musical.

Today, Jews still come from all over the world to this special land that was promised to Abraham. You can tell from many of our favorite foods where our people have lived throughout the world. Borscht, a beet soup, and my favorite, blintzes (stuffed crepes), are from Russia. We enjoy goulash from Hungary, and curries from India. But much of our food is typically Mediterranean, with many fruits, vegetables, and nuts. Falafel, stuffed Arabic pita bread, is to Israel what hamburgers are to you in America. My father was born in America, in New York City. He calls my mother and us kids his "sabras" because we were born in Israel. In Hebrew that means "prickly pears" or "the fruit of the cactus." Father says we are similar—tough and prickly on the outside, but when you get to know us, we are sweet and tender on the inside.

Israel is a tiny country at the eastern end of the Mediterranean Sea. It is about the size of your state of New Jersey. But there have been disputes and battles over the boundaries since the state of Israel was formed. Unlike the old Jewish nation, the new Israel has people of different nationalities and beliefs. Many Jews and Arabs want to live side by side, in peace. Many do not. It seems funny that in Hebrew, Jerusalem means "the city of peace." For so many years, though, it has not been peaceful at all. Father has taught us that there are important values in all religions and that we should all live our lives with responsibility, love, and thoughtfulness for each other. He says there are many paths and ways to the top of the mountain and we should respect them all. Our prophet Isaiah once had a dream of universal unity and peace. I hope and pray that his dream comes true soon.

Shalom. Peace, to you and your family,

Sarah Rebekah

mexico

Dear Pen Pal,

Buenos días. Hello. My name is María. I have two brothers and two sisters. My family and I live in Mexico City, the capital of the Republic of Mexico. We are the largest Spanish-speaking country in the world. Guatemala and Belize are our southern neighbors, and of course Los Estados Unidos, the United States, is our neighbor to the north.

I learned from your letter that we share something else besides our border—monarch butterflies! We call butterflies "mariposas." Mariposas fly as far as 1,500 kilometers from parts of the United States to nest high in the Sierra Madre Mountains outside of my city. The builders discovered them when they began to carve roads into the mountains. Biologists were afraid that logging in that area would destroy the mariposas' homes, so now 40 million acres have been put aside as a monarch butterfly reserve! That is also similar to your Monterey Bay reserve.

Mexico City is on the Central Plateau, the high valley within the Sierra Madre Mountains. Mexico has many mountains. We live near one of the highest, Mount Popocatépetl, a volcano. In Náhuatl, the language of the Aztecs, that means "smoking mountain." You might recognize these other Náhuatl words: coyoti, tomati, and chocolati. My Uncle Pedro is a farmer. He says our plateau has the best farmland in Mexico. He grows maiz (what you call corn) and wheat. Other crops grown in Mexico are vegetables, beans, rice, sugar cane, and cotton. These crops grow here all the time because we do not have a cold winter. It is like spring all year, with a rainy season from June to October. This year I saw coffee harvested for the first time. I did not know that coffee had to be picked by hand. Machines cannot tell the difference between green coffee beans and the ripe, red ones! And next time you get some chewing gum, think of us, because gum ("chicle") grows along our Gulf Coast on sapodilla trees.

Most of the people in our country are a mixture of Indian and Spanish. So is my family. We are Mestizos. That means we have both Indian and Spanish ancestors. Many different groups of Indians live here. They have their own customs and languages, but they also speak Spanish, our national language. Many Indians live much like their ancestors did in little villages far from cities. Indian women still wear long, colorful dresses and "rebozos," or shawls. The men wear "ponchos," or capes, and wide-brimmed hats called "sombreros." They come to town on market days to sell what they have made or grown. I especially like the toys they bring to

Christmas markets. Many children that live in country villages cannot go to school because there are not enough schools or teachers. Most children here in the city go to school through high school. I hope to study at the "universidad" to become a nurse or doctor. Then I can help the people who live far away from the big cities. Maybe I will be a teacher, I am not sure yet. I know I want to help others some way.

My papa makes beautiful "joyeria" (jewelry). Sometimes I go with him to market ("mercado") in the central square. I enjoy watching him work. I help him sell, take the money, and give back change. It makes me proud of my father when customers come up and say, "Your jewelry is beautiful!" We both reply, "Muchas gracias," thank you very much. Sometimes he makes a special bracelet or earrings for me! Papa said Mexico is sometimes called the "land of the handicrafts" because it is known for having skilled craftsmen. People come here to buy our colorful woven fabrics and baskets and the silver jewelry like Papa makes.

At the mercado people meet their friends and visit while they buy or sell their wares. Street musicians, called "mariachi" bands, play instruments and sing songs, which gives the mercado a very festive feeling. This is like your shopping mall, yes? It is fun seeing what other merchants have made, the clothes, leather goods, pottery, or hand-blown glass. Some "puestos" (stalls) have baskets filled with fruits and vegetables that farmers bring from the country, and there are many kinds of good food to eat. I love the warm conchas (bread) and the panaderia, or pastries. My favorite are sopapillas. They are deep-fried, then sprinkled with cinnamon and sugar. They are "bueno"!

In your letter, you said Mexican food is one of your favorite kinds of food. If you visit us, my mother will make homemade tortillas. We make them out of maiz or wheat flour. Then they are fried and eaten, as you would eat bread. We fill them with meat, sometimes chicken, sometimes beef or pork. If you add beans, cheese, and spices, you can make tacos or enchiladas. You probably already knew that! Did you know that at lunchtime here all the businesses and schools close for two to three hours? That is when we go home to eat lunch, our main meal of the day. Then everyone takes a "siesta," a nap. It is much too hot in the middle of the day to do anything else!

If you come here, I will take you to see the ruins of Teotihuacán, which means "place where gods are made." This ancient city was built thousands of years ago, right where we live now. I think in your letter you said that Indians used to live

where you live now? At school, we have been studying about the great early Indian civilizations, the Mayas and Aztecs. Our class took a trip to Teotihuacán. We climbed up hundreds of very steep stairs to the top of the Pyramid of the Sun. The view from the top was "magnifico"! It seemed like I could see forever. Our teacher said that these pyramids were built as temples to the gods and that they were so tall because they believed their gods—the sun, moon, wind, rain, and fire—were in the sky.

Some people say there is a festival somewhere in Mexico every day! On "fiestas," our feast days, churches are decorated with flowers and colored paper and there is a parade. All the townspeople and schoolchildren get dressed in fine clothes, and the little girls, like my younger sister Carolina, dress as angels in long, silk dresses with paper wings, and have flower wreaths in their hair. There is bell-ringing, music, dancing, and of course feasting! May is the month we celebrate mothers, and the most special mother to us is the Virgin Mary, the mother of Jesus. Every night in May, the girls dress in white dresses and we take flowers to the church for Mary. We call it Ofrecer Flores. In Mexico, when girls turn 15, they celebrate with a very big party. It is called the Quinceañera. The birthday girl wears a beautiful white gown, like a bride. She and her date are escorted by 14 girls and 14 boys, and there is a big dance and a feast. Is this like your sweet 16? My sister Teresa will have her 15th birthday in July. She is very excited and a little nervous too.

Every year on Guadalupe Day, 12 December, we take a special journey to visit a very sacred shrine outside our city. In 1531, Juan Diego, an Indian peasant, was part of a miracle. On Tepayac Hill, the Virgin Mary appeared to him. In his Náhuatl language, she told him to pick roses from a place where, he knew, nothing but cactus grew. He was to take the roses to the bishop and tell him that he had seen the Mother of God and that she wanted a church built there. Diego went to see the bishop and when he opened his cape, roses fell at his feet. On the inside of his cape you could see the Virgin Mary's image on the cloth. I believe this story because I have seen the cape with her image with my own eyes. The cape, or "tilma," of Diego is on display at the church that was built for Mary, our Virgin of Guadalupe. So every year on her day, we go to mass at this church.

At Christmastime, we celebrate Las Posadas. This is a parade that acts out the search Mary and Joseph made to find an inn ("posada") where the baby Jesus was

born. Afterwards, there is always a piñata party for the children. A "piñata" is a paper jar decorated with colored paper to look like an animal, a person, or some curious object. It is filled with treats and hung from the ceiling, and then children who are blindfolded try to break it with a long stick. When someone finally breaks the piñata, we all race to get the goodies that scatter to the ground.

I am Catholic and go to church every Sunday. At mass last week, the priest said that we should be aware of how wonderful the world around us is. He said we should take pleasure in what life has to offer and appreciate what we have. That made me think of how much in this world is amazing to me. I wonder about our smoking mountains and how the mariposas know how to fly from your country to mine. Why are we who we are, and why are we here? I have wondered about Tepayac, where Diego had his vision and the roses. And guess what? Tepayac is the same place where the Aztecs worshipped their earth goddess, Tonantzin (that means "mother" in Náhuatl). The Indians loved her very much. Does that make you wonder? Two stories about two sacred mothers on the same site. I do not think it matters if we stand on top of a pyramid, inside a church, or even on a street corner in Mexico City, we should appreciate and give thanks for all of the people and places in the world.

Come visit us. "Mi casa es su casa," my house is your house.

Adios, amigo. Good-bye, my friend,

Maria

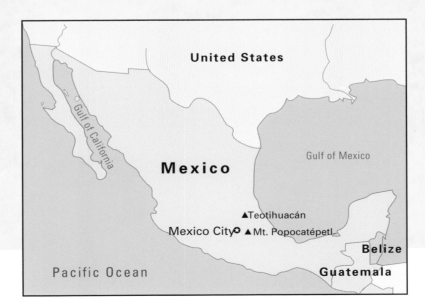

scotland

Dear Pen Pal,

Hello. My name is Cameron and I'm from Scotland. It was great fun getting your letter and hearing about you and your life. When I pass by someone's home, I always wonder what the people inside are like. And yes! I do think we are more alike than different. Robert Burns, a famous Scottish poet, wrote a poem that I think means we should all try to get along better. It goes like this: "Man to man the/whole world o'er (over)/shall brothers be/for a'(all) that!" What do you think?

This is a good place to tell you about my own history. On my father's side we are the Campbells, one of the great "clans" (families) of the northern Highlands. The Highlands make up more than two-thirds of Scotland. It is where you would see the most spectacular scenery. There are rocky peaks, islands along the coasts, valleys of forests (called "glens"), and the rolling "moors" (hills), which are covered in purple heather. The Scottish clansmen wore kilts, or knee-length pleated skirts, made from their own woolen "tartan" (a plaid pattern) that showed which clan they were from. Our family tartan is a plaid of black, red, blue, and yellow. Today, tartans are also made into a variety of clothing, like ties, shirts, or hats. A few Scotsmen still wear their kilts every day, but the men in my family (my father, grandfather, and myself) save our kilts for special occasions or festivals. When I wear my kilt it makes me feel close to my Scottish culture.

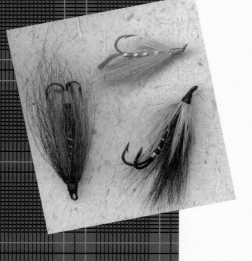

My father and I enjoy fishing. The Highlands have many "lochs," or lakes. Fishing is sort of a Campbell tradition. My grandfather took my dad, and now my dad takes me. I sent you some fishing flies I made myself. Fishing is also an important industry in Scotland, but in our family we enjoy it simply for the sport. Sometimes we go to the little fishing village of Crail, which is a popular resort on the east coast, but mostly we fish nearby. I'm sure you have heard of the Loch Ness Monster. Hundreds of people claim they have seen this huge creature. Affectionately, we call her Nessie. Urquhart Castle, a stone ruin, juts out into Loch Ness and is a perfect observation point for Nessie seekers. I have been through the Nessie exhibition in Drumnadrochit. There are some very serious scientific opinions about our world-famous monster. I don't know if I believe it or not, but I must admit that whenever I am sitting in a fishing boat on Loch Ness, I am always looking over my shoulder, hoping to see her. On the news the

other day, I saw that in Japan there have been sightings of a similar creature. They call their monster Ishi. Maybe they are related!

Our capital city, Edinburgh, is in the central part of Scotland called the Lowlands. Most Scots live around the Lowlands because there are jobs here. Did you know that 40 percent of the computers used in Europe come from here? We have some Macintosh (good Scottish name, aye?) computers in school, but I don't have one at home yet.

In southern Scotland, called the Borders, there are good pastures for raising sheep. There are many woolen mills and factories there that make the wool into clothing. You can find sheep in all the rural areas of our country! (Sometimes, I think the sheep believe that the roads were made just for them!) It's a good thing we make so much wool, because even the summers here are cool and the winters are very cold. We wear thick sweaters and tweed coats all year 'round!

I live in Edinburgh. The new city is built around the old city. Our most famous land-marks are Edinburgh Castle, which sits upon Castle Rock, which overlooks the city, and the Palace of Holyrood. This was once the home of Mary, Queen of Scots. If you were to come here, I would take you there to see a parade led by pipers that passes the castle gates. We could also visit the Royal Botanic Gardens, which are quite lovely. Or perhaps, since you like music, we would go to the Edinburgh Festival of the Arts, which happens every August. It is a great celebration of art, music, drama, and even comedy.

Edinburgh has been a centre of literature and learning since the 18th century. The University of Edinburgh is over 400 years old! My parents went to college there. Now, my father is a book publisher and my mother teaches English literature. So you see, books are important in my family too. You can learn so much from books about people and the different places they live. I am glad to know you also like to read. Sometimes I get lost in my books. My favourite Scottish authors are Robert Louis Stevenson and Sir Arthur Conan Doyle. Stevenson wrote *Treasure Island* and *Kidnapped*. I read some-where that Stevenson lived for some time on the Monterey Peninsula. Did you know that? And Doyle created Sherlock Holmes! The *Hounds of the Baskervilles* is my favourite of his mysteries. I still get shivers when I think of that dog with the haunting sound in the misty moors! Another famous Scottish author was J.M. Barrie. You would probably know him best from his play *Peter Pan*.

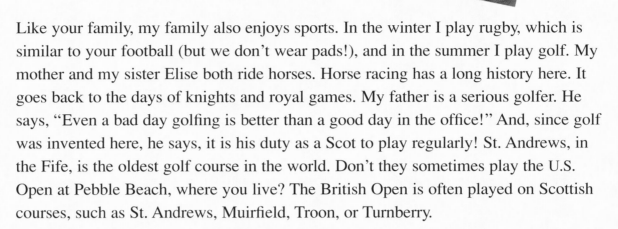

Like your family, my family also enjoys sports. In the winter I play rugby, which is similar to your football (but we don't wear pads!), and in the summer I play golf. My mother and my sister Elise both ride horses. Horse racing has a long history here. It goes back to the days of knights and royal games. My father is a serious golfer. He says, "Even a bad day golfing is better than a good day in the office!" And, since golf was invented here, he says, it is his duty as a Scot to play regularly! St. Andrews, in the Fife, is the oldest golf course in the world. Don't they sometimes play the U.S. Open at Pebble Beach, where you live? The British Open is often played on Scottish courses, such as St. Andrews, Muirfield, Troon, or Turnberry.

When it comes to music, Scotland is quite well known for its bagpipes. No other musical instrument looks or sounds quite like them. My uncle plays them and has explained to me how it is done. Blowing into the mouthpiece fills the bag with air, which then fills the pipes, which then make the sound. As proud as I am of my ancestry, to tell you the truth, I would much rather listen to rock music on my stereo! Of course, the most famous British band of all time is the Beatles. I have all of their albums (they were my Mum and Dad's). The Beatles were from Liverpool, England, but I think Paul McCartney sometimes lives on Mull of Kintyre, an island off the coast of Scotland.

We are English on my mother's side. Scotland, England, Wales, and Northern Ireland make up the United Kingdom of Great Britain. For short, we call it the U.K. or Britain. It is also known as the British Isles because there are over 800 islands. On holiday we visit my grandparents, who live in England, outside of London. When we were little, Grandfather Phillips would take us on the red double-decker bus, and we would go sightseeing around London. We went past Big Ben, the Tower of London, Westminster Abbey (that is where the royal coronations take place), Scotland Yard (headquarters for the British police), and Number 10 Downing Street (the home of the prime minister). Then we stopped to see the changing of the guard at Buckingham Palace, where Queen Elizabeth, lives with what is left of her family.

Now that we are older, we enjoy going to plays and concerts. *Les Miserables* and *The Phantom of the Opera* are favourites of mine, while Mother and Elise enjoy going to the Royal Ballet. There is always so much to do in London. But my grandfather and I always take time to visit the exhibits at the British Museum. He and I share an interest in archaeology. The exhibits there make the history I have studied in school seem

real to me. I have actually seen Egyptian mummies and the Rosetta Stone, which made it possible for scientists to translate a forgotten language.

Next holiday, Grandfather and I are planning a trip to Wiltshire, England, to see Stonehenge. It is one of many ancient structures that have been built to face the sunrise or moonrise at certain times of the year. Debates go on about whether these mysterious places were built as observatories for early astronomers to watch the sky, or as religious temples. Why did the people of long ago spend so much time and energy moving these great, heavy rocks into formations, and then what were they used for? Stonehenge is on the United Nations' list of places to be protected for the earth's cultural and national heritage. Somewhat like the protection of your Monterey Bay and your national parks. Surely you know it was a Scotsman, John Muir, who started your national parks. He was from Dunbar, Scotland. Some other places on the U.N. list are the Egyptian Pyramids, Machu Picchu in Peru, the Vatican in Rome, and Israel's Holy City, Jerusalem. I think it is great when countries work together to protect these special sites. It's a good step toward mutual respect of different people and their cultures.

But sometimes I just don't understand why people act the way they do. If religion is supposed to teach us to love one another, how come there are so many religious wars, like the ones in Ireland or in the Middle East? Why can't people live together peacefully? John Lennon was my favourite Beatle, and the message in his song "Imagine" is perfect: "Imagine there's nothing to kill or die for . . . Imagine all the people, living life in peace. You might say I'm a dreamer, but I'm not the only one. I hope someday you'll join us, and the world will live as one." Perhaps I'm one of those dreamers Lennon sang about. It sounds to me that you are too. We can both imagine the world a better place. Maybe we will be the ones to grow up and help make it happen.

Let's give peace a chance!

Yours Sincerely,

Cameron

france

Dear Pen Pal,

Bonjour. Hello from France! My name is André. I live in Paris. So I am not only French, but also Parisian. People from everywhere love to come to Paris, the City of Lights. Why is it called the City of Lights? Perhaps it is because it shines like a diamond, especially the Place de la Concorde. Or maybe because we had the first street lights. Others believe that Paris is a city of learning and sheds light as knowledge. Is that why people come? I do not know. If it is because Paris is so beautiful, or because it is a center of art and learning, or because it is the fashion capital of the world, I cannot tell you. People simply come.

I would like to tell you about the Eiffel Tower. It was built for the 1889 Paris exhibition and was named after Alexandre Gustave Eiffel, the engineer who designed it. The Eiffel Tower may seem especially tall because we do not have many skyscrapers in the heart of Paris, like you do in your cities. Instead, the tallest buildings are located in one area, called La Defense, on the western edge of Paris. From the top of the Eiffel tower you can see all of Paris. I love to look at Notre Dame, the Gothic cathedral that sits on the Ile de la Cité, in the River Seine. Paris began as a fishing village on that little island 2,000 years ago! That is so difficult to imagine!

You wrote that you like to think about your history. As I walk in Paris past statues of famous French people, I imagine them walking on these same streets, passing many of the same buildings, hundreds of years before me. I can feel the history under my feet. When I see the Arc de Triomphe that Napoleon built, I wonder what Paris was like when Napoleon was a boy. I read that when Napoleon was 15 years old he went to a military school, where the other boys teased him because he was so small. Perhaps it was this teasing that made him work so hard to be better. Imagine, our history may have been quite different, if Napoleon had been tall.

If you could see all of France from the top of the Eiffel Tower, this is what you would see: the Pyrenees Mountains in the west, towards Spain; the Alps to the east; the Riviera, with its famous resorts, to the south; and farmland to the north. My cousins, Michelle and Pierre, live in the north, in Normandy, near the English Channel. They live in a stone farmhouse. Normandy is the cattle and dairy land of France. It is where my favorite cheese, Camembert, is made. It is "trés bien" (very good)! Cities and regions in France are known for the products that they make or grow. In Dijon they make spicy moutard (French for mustard), and the Bordeaux and Burgundy regions are known for fine wines. French people are so proud of their wine that at the end of every summer there is a festival, "fête de la vigne," where they celebrate the harvest of the grapes.

The French also make many kinds of bread. Perhaps it is because we eat bread with every meal. Each morning I go to the bakery to buy baguettes (long, skinny

loaves) or croissants for breakfast. We eat them warm from the oven with butter and jam, and with a cup of café au lait (for me it is a little bit of hot coffee and a lot of hot milk!). Telling you about food is making me very hungry! It is said that the French enjoy cooking, as much as we do eating! You would love all the pastry shops we have. Oh, la la! So many delicious pâtisseries…chocolate macaroons, petit fours, tartes, and eclair au chocolat!

I try to ride my bike almost everywhere. Many people do, unless they take the Metro (subway). Some people do not drive because the traffic is so bad in Paris and because our streets are not very wide. Some streets are only for walking. No bicycles, no mopeds, no cars!

Sports are very popular in France. The biggest sports event we have is a bicycle race called the Tour de France. In fact, it is the most important bicycle race in the world. Do you know it? An American, Greg Lamonde, has won three times. The cyclists ride all over France for almost a month! Mon Dieu! I like to play "le football," or soccer, with my friends. Tennis is also popular. Did you know that tennis was invented by French priests? My entire family enjoys skiing when we go on holiday in the winter. Many French children who ski dream of skiing in the Olympics. They hope to follow the great downhill skier, Jean Claude Killy. He won three gold medals in the 1968 Olympics! He was "trés magnifique"!

I think you would love Paris. If you came, we could visit many museums. The Louvre is my favorite. You walk through a glass pyramid to get inside! We would have our "dejeuner" (lunch) at my parents' café. And I am sure you would think the Champ Elysées is the most beautiful boulevard in all the world. It is lined with chestnut trees; "trés chic" stores and hotels; large universities, theaters, and churches; and also royal palaces with towers. Paris has many parks too. When I was a young boy, I especially liked the Parc Monceau. It has a carousel with not only horses, but also coaches, motorcycles, a bus, a fire engine, and a rocket ship!

Now that I am older, I have less time to go to the park. I go to school until 6:00 p.m. We take two hours for lunch, then go to eat with our families, study, or sometimes visit friends. There is no school on Wednesday afternoons or on Sundays. On those days, and after school, I help at the café with my sister Nicole. I love the café and the wonderful smells that come from the kitchen. I want to be a Grand Chef de Cuisine. In France it is a great honor to be a chef in a top restaurant. It will take much training, but Father says that if I work very hard, like Napoleon, it can happen.

Many interesting people come into the café. French people spend hours sitting and talking, long after I've cleared their dishes. But I especially like to hear visitors from other countries speaking different languages. I would love to visit every

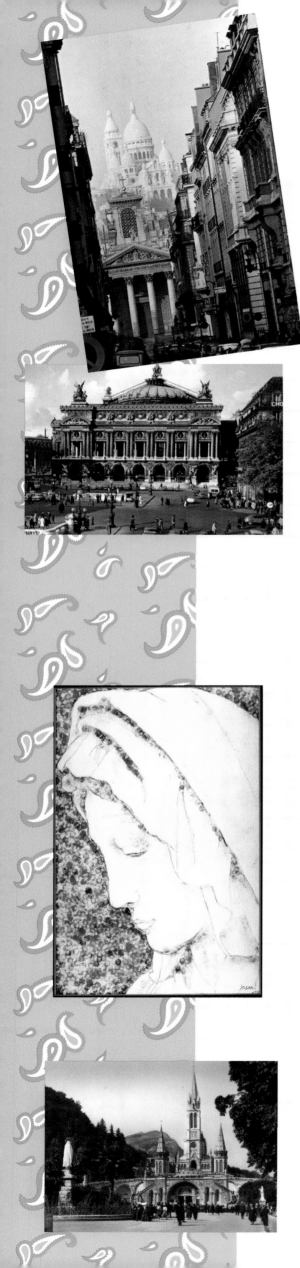

country in the world, like they do at "It's a Small World" at Euro Disney. Would you not like that too? Think of the new friends we would meet! Speaking of friends, you said you visited the Statue of Liberty in New York. Did you know she was a gift from France? Two countries reached across the ocean in friendship, just like us.

In your letter you said you are interested in angels. Our museums and cathedrals are full of paintings, stained-glass windows, and sculptures of angels. You must see the dome of the Paris Opera House. Chagall painted a heavenly orchestra of angels. Their bodies are cellos and other musical instruments that dance across the ceiling. I am a Catholic. We believe that each of us has at least one guardian angel who sits on our shoulder and helps us make good choices. I have read stories in the Bible about angels. An angel appeared to the Virgin Mary and the shepherds to announce the birth of her baby, Jesus. Our French saint, Francisca, said she could see her guardian angel at midnight and could read from his glow!

You know, there is a holy site in France at Lourdes. It is said that over 100 years ago the Virgin Mary appeared to Bernadette, a 14-year-old girl. Mary told her to dig a hole. And from that hole came healing waters from the rock. Supposedly, thousands of people have been cured at Lourdes. My mother told me that Mary has also appeared to some children in Medjugorje, in what used to be Yugoslavia. The first time she came was in 1981, on what is now known as Apparition Hill. She has continued to appear every day since, at 5:40 p.m. She asks people to pray more and learn to respect all religions. She wants us to love each other. Maybe it is working. Every day, thousands of people from all over the world go to this place to see this happen.

I believe that if angels and miracles could happen in the past, then they could be happening now. And maybe, if we hope for good things and believe in miracles, we will get what we ask for. It is "a small world after all," and we need to take care of it and each other.

Au revoir. Good-bye,

ANDRÉ

peru

Dear Pen Pal,

Hola. My name is Juan. I live with my parents and three brothers in the high country of Perú in South America. Perú is on the same continent as California, just much farther south. It was very exciting to get your letter from North America! You have taught me about you, and now I will tell you about me and my life in Perú.

Your town is by the sea, but mine is up high in the Andes Mountains. Sometimes it takes quite a while to get used to our altitude. Perú has some of the tallest peaks in the world. Many have snow on them all year, and the climate in the "montañas" is much cooler than in other parts of South America. We do not have tidepools to explore, but I love to explore caves and climb rocks on our high plateaus. Some nights it seems as if the stars are so close that I can reach out and touch them! On my last birthday, my parents gave me a telescope because they know how much I love to study the sky. One day, while looking through my telescope, I saw a condor! That is not a common sight! Condors are huge birds that live high in the rocks of our mountains.

We have also a dog, Rubio, a cat named José, some chickens, a couple of "cabras" (goats), and a pet llama. Everyone here has at least one llama. They are native to the Andes. Because our mountains are so steep, the people here tame them to carry things, as well as alpacas and "huanacos," which are similar. Llamas can be very stubborn; if you put even one milligram too much on their backs, they sit down! My mother also spins the llama's hair into yarn that she weaves into fabric and then makes into clothes, like "rebozos" (shawls) and "serapes," the woolen blankets we wear as ponchos. Mother and her friends spin wool into yarn on a spindle while they are walking and talking. They also sell the yarn and fabric they make at the "mercado," our marketplace.

My friends and I like going to the movies too. We have two theaters in my town. Sometimes we get American films that have been translated into Spanish. I like it when Arnold Schwarzenegger says, "Hasta la vista, baby!" I especially enjoy adventures in space, like the *Star Wars* and *Star Trek* movies. Not all families here have televisions, but everyone owns a radio. I listen to Peruvian and American music. Traditional Peruvian music is played with drums, a "quena" (a type of flute), rattles, and a small harp.

I also like to read, and I do very well in school. You wrote that your brother plays baseball. Here we play "futbol," like your soccer. My younger brother, Umberto, he is a fanatic! He would rather play futbol than go to school, or even eat! He dreams only of being the next Pelé, the greatest soccer player of all time (even if he is from Brazil!). He played many times at the National Stadium in Lima, our capital, when my father was studying at the University of San Marcos. This university is the oldest in South America. My father says

that doing well in athletics is one way to be successful, but getting a good education is the most important thing that will help us get the good life we dream of. My father is a high-school history teacher. From him I have learned much about my ancestors, the Incas.

The Incas were a powerful empire from about 1300 A.D. to 1533 A.D. Our city of Cuzco, which means "navel" in Quechua (the Inca language), was considered the center, or capital, of the empire. Seven million Indians live in Perú today. Many live in villages high in the Andes, very much as their ancestors did. Farming is the main industry of Perú. The farmland near Cuzco is the highest in the world. Ancient Inca farmers terraced the montaña slopes for growing, and built reservoirs to irrigate these hillside farms. They grew wheat, "maize" (corn), and potatoes. Potatoes once grew wild in the highlands, but the Incas were the first to cultivate them. They grew over 200 kinds.

According to Inca legend, Manco Capac, the first Inca ruler, was sent to earth to spread civilization. He rose from Lake Titicaca carrying a golden rod, and then he walked to Cuzco to make it the center of the empire. The early Incas knew much about the stars and planets, and they built their temples to face the sun. Our Church of Santo Domingo is built next to Coricancha, the Temple of the Sun. You can see the old and new buildings in the photograph I sent. When the temple was discovered, it was covered in gold! It is said that the Inca ruler would sit there on the throne each morning to greet the sun. Incas believed gold was the sun's tears. The Incas celebrated the harvest with the Feast of the Sun. At dawn, they kissed the first rays of sun on the Plaza de Armas, which is still the main plaza in Cuzco. Then they feasted, played music, and danced the rest of the day, like we do at our fiestas today.

It is said that a solid-gold fence once surrounded our entire plaza! And when the Spanish conquerors came, the Incas hid the golden fence in Lake Titicaca. It has never been found (the lake is very deep and is also the highest lake in the world). When the Inca ruler was captured, he promised that if he was released, he would give the Spanish leader a roomful of gold! The Spanish leader agreed, but after the Inca ruler gave him the gold, the Spaniard killed him anyway. The Spanish conquerors only wanted gold. They did not care about the Inca civilization or their accomplishments. Minerals are still mined in our montañas, but it is nothing compared to the gold and silver that was taken back to Europe by the Spaniards.

I always go with my father when he takes his history classes to see the ruins of Machu Picchu, once a great city and fortress. If you came here I would take you there. My father says Machu Picchu is now considered the eighth wonder of the world. To me, the real wonder is, how did they build such a city on top of the montañas with such huge blocks of granite? Some weigh more than 100 tons each and had to be cut with stone tools! And how were they carried and fitted perfectly into place without any machinery? The Incas must have been very good stone carvers. Machu Picchu seems to sit on top of the world. Along the mountain road leading up to it, there are signs that say, Watch for UFOs! I know visitors come from all over the world to see these ruins, but from all over the universe as well? I have

not seen a UFO myself, at least not yet, but many locals say they have. Maybe the mysterious lights often seen at Machu Picchu really are from extraterrestrial spacecraft! Our ancestors did worship the earth and sky and believed that their kings and queens came from the heavens! Maybe these cities on top of the high peaks, and the roads and lines cut into the earth, were built for these visitors from outer space.

Oh! I haven't even told you about the lines! They are called the Nazca lines because archaeologists believe that they were made by the Nazca people who lived in the desert, along the southern coast of Perú, from about 200 B.C. to 600 A.D. Some of the lines are straight and up to 3 kilometers long; others are huge triangles and other geometric forms; and some are enormous, realistic drawings of animals such as spiders and hummingbirds. The photo I sent you is called Spaceman. Why did these ancient people use the earth as their drawing board? The lines only look like pictures when seen from the air! Since the Nazcas could not fly, why were they there? Except for some pottery and artwork, these lines are all that is left of this very mysterious civilization.

Ancient sites and sacred landscapes are among the wonders of the world, like your marine sanctuary in Monterey. I believe it is very important that scientists and archaeologists from around the world work together to save these monuments and artifacts of the past; they might help us understand our native cultures. My father has made history seem alive for me by studying these early civilizations. I read your letter to my friends. We all want to help make a difference in our world! And I agree with you. If we learn more about each other, we will see how similar we are. Maybe then, peace will come through understanding our differences and appreciating how we are the same.

Adios and paz. Good-bye and peace,

Juan

nigeria

Dear Pen Pal,

Hello. My name is Enole. I am Nigerian. Nigeria is in the huge continent of Africa. Thank you so much for writing. I took your letter to school to read to all of my friends! We were all very excited!

Would you like to visit us? Nigeria is very friendly. When strangers come to visit, we give them something to eat and drink. I am always interested in what they have to say. It is a custom to give them fruit or sugarcane when they leave. I wish, some-times, that I could go with them. There are so many places I want to see. I would love to visit you in California.

You wrote about the tall pine trees and animals in your backyard. If you visited me, you would see thick rain forests. Trees over 60 meters tall tower over us like huge umbrellas. The animals in my backyard, besides our dog and the chickens, are the many tropical birds and monkeys that live in the treetops. Nigeria is in the western part of Africa. Because Nigeria's northern border touches the southern edge of the great Sahara Desert, and our southern border is near the equator, my country has several climates: desert, rain forest, swamp forest, and "savanna" (grassland). Our weather is tropical, so we have two seasons: a warm, dry one and a warm, wet one!

In my family there are me, my parents, my sister, and my two brothers (that's us in the picture I sent). My cousin and aunt also live with us. I enjoy school too, like you, and I love to dance. Traditional dancing is very popular here. My brothers play soccer. We live in a house in the city of Onitsha. Onitsha is modern. We have televi-sions, movie theaters, cars, factories, and offices, like the one my mother works in. My mother is a secretary for an oil company. On Saturdays, my cousin and I help my aunt in her fabric stall at·the market. She sells the fabrics she has woven in beautiful colors from fine cotton threads. Your shopping mall seems a bit like our market. Ours is outside, though, in a large, open space, with covered stalls all around it. You can buy products there from all over the world. Besides shopping, we also go to market to visit with friends and get the latest news.

Part of the fun of the market is to argue over prices with the women, like my aunt, who run the stalls. We call them "market mammies." They are so good at what they do that some are very rich and live in big houses with servants! There's also enter-tainment—jugglers, dancers, and musicians. At the snack bars you can buy foods that you know, like ice cream. If you were here, you would discover many different

kinds of food to eat. How about fried locust? (Locust is a kind of grasshopper.) Or foo foo, a dough made from corn flour? We eat foo foo with spicy sauce and red peppers or with garri. Garri is fried cassava, a root vegetable like yams or potatoes. We also eat chicken, duck, and goat, but hedgehog meat and giant watersnake are delicious too! At the market, there are baskets of fruits and vegetables and other foods that farmers grow. There are mangoes, rice, plantains (like bananas), sugar-cane, coffee, groundnuts (peanuts), and cocoa beans. We use cocoa beans to make cocoa and chocolate, and groundnuts to make oil for cooking. Peanuts are called groundnuts because they grow under the ground! I eat them by the handful! At the market, bags of groundnuts are stacked in huge pyramids.

The capital of our country used to be Lagos, but now it is Abuja. Lagos is the largest city south of the Sahara. It is much bigger than Onitsha; over a million people live there! Lagos had electric street lights even before there were any in London! There are lots of buildings, stores, and cars, like in your big cities, but you'll also see carts (we call them "lorries" or "mammy wagons") that carry people and their goods to market. In Nigeria people carry things on their heads—parcels, pots, baskets, almost anything! We can even run and play games without our schoolbooks falling off our heads.

In Nigeria there are modern cities, but there are also villages in the forest where people have lived the same way for thousands of years. My father was raised in such a village on the Niger River. Nigeria is named for this river. When we visit my grandparents and relatives on the river, we always take a river bus, but you could take a canoe. Along the banks of the river, we pass banana palms and swamps with mangrove trees. "Creek people" build their houses on stilts along the river. They step directly off their porches onto their fishing boats. Their children learn to swim before they can walk! I wouldn't mind swimming with lizards, but I don't like snakes (except as food of course!).

My grandparents' house, like all the others in the village, is small and square. All the houses are built very close to each other. They make them by weaving together wood and vines like a basket, a very big basket. (They don't use nails because the rain would rust them away.) Then they plaster the house with clay and cover the

roof with banana leaves. Women wash, cook, and work in their small vegetable gardens. The men farm the land. When we visit, I help my cousins feed their animals (pigs, chickens, ducks, goats, and sheep) and carry water from the stream in large buckets—on our heads, of course! There are no telephones or telegraphs in the villages, so when we are there, we hear special messages from the "talking drums." Drummers communicate by beating messages on hollow logs that are heard by people in the other villages. It's musical too!

Our music might sound strange to you. It is mostly for dancing. The drum is our main instrument and gives the beat, or rhythm, for the dancers. Xylophones, and string and wind instruments, are also popular. Dancing is an important part of our culture and celebrations. Sometimes we wear masks and costumes while we dance that help tell our tribal stories and legends. But a dance can start for any reason. You might dance for someone who has returned home, or for someone's success, or simply for the fun of it!

Like your country, we have many different people in Nigeria. We have four main groups: the Fulani, the Hausas, the Ibo, and the Yorubas. But there are about 250 different tribal groups in Nigeria. Each tribe has its own dances, dress, customs, and language. Our radio programs are broadcast in 15 languages! Sometimes, though, it is difficult for young children who are starting school. You see, we all speak our own language at home. But since English is our national language, when we go to school we have to learn our lessons in this new language as well!

My people are the Ibo and most of us live east of the Niger River. The Ibo are primarily farmers. Many Ibos wear clothes like yours in America, especially those of us who live in a city, but many still dress traditionally. Both men and women wear long skirts. We make them by wrapping a long piece of cloth around ourselves several times and tying the end in a knot. Mothers wear a wide piece of cloth, called an "oja," around their waists to carry their babies. Women and girls wear brightly colored turbans, called "gele," that they tie a certain way so the ends stand up.

Many Nigerians still hold tribal beliefs, such as worshipping spirits and the nature gods. But my family is Christian; most Ibos and Yorubas are. The Yorubas live mainly in the southwest and are also farmers. Yoruba men wear long, beautifully embroidered garments, and the women wear skirts similar to ours. The Yorubas are friendly and very proud of their long history. They say their ancestors came from Egyptian kingdoms. Their techniques for wood carving and making bronze artwork

haven't changed since the time of ancient Egypt. The oldest known African sculptures were found in central Nigeria. They were terra cotta figures created by the Nok civilization around 500 B.C.

My father says that Ibo people like to learn. If an Ibo student doesn't win a scholarship, his entire family works to pay for his studies. My father's village helped send him to the University at Ibaden. There is an old African proverb: "It takes a whole village to raise a child." Now my father teaches other students who have come from similar villages. He says it is his way of giving back. I want to be a teacher too. Many college graduates in our country become teachers because many are needed here in Nigeria and in other parts of Africa. We are proud that more Nigerian children go to school than children in any other African country. Father says we are Africa's hope.

I agree with you that we can be teachers to each other. I have learned from you how similar we are, yet our differences make us interesting. The people of Africa are starting to work together too. For example, African people are uniting to save the animals that are in danger of becoming extinct. Before, many animals were killed or captured for money. If we can't protect these magnificent creatures, how can we hope to save ourselves? I believe that we're all part of a master plan or painting. In the big painting, the creator carefully chose the colors of each bird's feathers and made each zebra's pattern unique. He also made each person an individual, from our faces to our fingertips. My hope is that we can learn to appreciate the beauty of the finished painting, with all its variations, and allow everyone to be as free and happy as we were meant to be.

Have you ever had a kola nut? It's like a green grapefruit, filled with juicy nuts, that you chew when you are thirsty. Coca-Cola is made from them! If you visited me, I would give you one. It is a sign of friendship.

With Friendship,

Enole

russia

Dear Pen Pal,

Zdrastvuite. Greetings. My name is Elina. I am Russian. My family—my parents, my older brother Nicholai, and Babushka, my granny—lives in St. Petersburg. I was very excited to get your letter and am eager to learn about people from other countries. It was interesting to read about your family and the way you live, and also about Samantha Smith. For such a young girl to write to our president! She was truly an ambassador of peace! Samantha's letter and visit may have helped President Yuri Andropov change his thinking about how our country fits with the rest of the world. Who would know this?

Before 1992, Russia was part of the USSR (Union of Soviet Socialist Republics), or the Soviet Union. It was a huge country. The people who lived in the Soviet Union were of 100 different nationalities, speaking 60 different languages! My parents once took a trip on the Trans-Siberian Railroad. They traveled from Moscow to the Port of Vladivostok. The trip was 9,300 kilometers and took an entire week, one way! They traveled through eight time zones. What was once the USSR is now 15 independent republics. But the Russian Republic, where I live, is still the largest country in the world.

Most Russian people live in the steppe region. This is where the industrial cities are and also where most of the farming is. North of the steppe are thick forests; this region is called the "taiga." Fishermen, hunters, and lumbermen live here. But it is also home to bears, wolves, fox, ermine, beavers, and reindeer! Some people, Eskimos and others, live along the coast of the Arctic Ocean on the treeless plain of the frozen tundra. They fish, breed reindeer, and hunt to make their living. Russia is very, very cold in the winter. There is one area, Verhoyansk, that has the coldest temperature in the world: -51 degrees centigrade (-60 Fahrenheit)! Our winters are long too. We always need to wear a warm coat and hat. That is probably why we enjoy eating many different kinds of soup. Uha is a fish soup, borscht is made of beets, and rassolnick is made from meat and pickled cucumbers. I especially love syrniki, patties made from soft cheese, flour, and egg, which we serve with jam and sour cream. My babushka makes the very best nalistniki. First, she fills crepes with meat or mushrooms, and then she fries them. They are also served with sour cream. Russian people eat a great deal of sour cream.

Russian people also love to read. This is maybe so because it is so cold much of the time, we cannot go outside. Instead, we put a big blanket on ourselves and enjoy a good book. My favorite right now is *Tom Sawyer*, by Mark Twain.

I have only read this in Russian. Our father of literature is Aleksandr Pushkin. He was a great poet. We honor him and others on Poet's Day. With the changes in Russia now, we have so many choices of books to read than before.

Change is everywhere in my country. For example, when my parents were growing up (and most of my life), our city was called Leningrad, after a political leader, Lenin. Recently, we voted to change it back to St. Petersburg, or Peter's City, after its founder, Peter the Great. Voting is not new for us. But now, people have a choice who to vote for. How we vote is just one change we are experiencing as we move from communism to democracy. We are building a new government "of the people," but change is hard. Some things are troublesome, like empty stores or long lines for food. But we are hopeful. Before, if we disagreed with a leader, we could not vote him out of office, or write about it in the newspaper, or ask any questions. Now, our opinion makes a difference. The statue of Lenin that stood in our city has been removed. Lenin is off his pedestal! He, and all he stood for, has been replaced with a statue of Peter the Great. It is a symbol of new hope for our future.

St. Petersburg is a beautiful city! It looks like it was brought here from Europe because its designers were European. Some visitors say it is a Russian Venice because it is also built on islands with bridges that cross canals. Our apartment looks over a canal. St. Petersburg is on the Gulf of Finland. Peter considered it his "window on the West." But after 1917, when the czars were overthrown, a curtain went over his window and we could no longer look at the West. Communication with the rest of the world ended.

For 75 years the cloud of communism hung over the Soviet Union. The government owned the land, the factories, the banks, and the stores. Farmers lived on "kolkhoz" and "sovkhoz," collective state farms where people shared the work, and supposedly the profits. It did not always seem so, though. The government told us what we could read, write, say, and think! Our people had a lot of fear and little personal freedom. We had beautiful churches, mosques, and cathedrals, like St. Catherine's Cathedral, but they were not for praying. You could visit them as museums only. The government forced everyone to be atheists, people who do not believe in God. Babushka's family was Russian Orthodox before Communism. Now we can go to church. My family celebrated Christmas openly for the first time in 1991. My babushka cried. She said they were tears of happiness because the iron curtain had opened and now there would be change.

Moscow is the largest city in Russia. It is the capital and heart of the country. When we are in Moscow, Mother and I go shopping at GUM. This is the largest

department store in Russia. It is five stories tall and very beautiful. In Moscow, we always take a walk in Red Square. As we pass the Kremlin and St. Basil's Cathedral, with its domes that look like onions, I feel like I am walking back in history. I get the same feeling at the Hermitage, the winter palace of the czar. Now the Hermitage is an art museum. The building is a work of art, and worth seeing even if it did not have famous masterpieces hanging on its walls.

Last Easter, Babushka took me to the Hermitage to see the famous egg collection by Fabergé! Peter Fabergé was Russia's most famous jeweler. He was born in St. Petersburg, but his work was known all over the world. His most famous pieces are the Easter eggs he made for the czars, with miniature jeweled family portraits, or tiny yachts, or royal coaches that fit inside golden eggs.

You wrote that you have an angel collection. I have a collection too. I have 11 sets of Matreshka dolls, one for each birthday. Each set has several brightly painted wooden dolls that get smaller and smaller and fit inside each other. They are very typical of our folk art. The peasant doll I sent you is also Russian folk art and is made not far from my home.

I have no real artistic talent myself. Not like my friend Oleg. He can draw any-thing. In Russia, children like Oleg who have special talent make a choice when they are young to go to special schools. My brother Nicholai loves ice skating. He goes to the sports school, where my father coaches ice hockey. Our fathers are both coaches! Nicholai has already competed in the National Sport Olympiada for schoolchildren. I take ballet classes for exercise and because I love to dance. But my friend Katja is a very beautiful dancer and attends a school of ballet. She dreams of dancing like Maya Plisetskaya for the Bolshoi Theater in Moscow. Russia is considered the home of classical ballet. My favorite ballets are *Swan Lake* and *The Nutcracker,* with the beautiful music by Tchaikovsky. There have been many famous Russian composers and authors. Now, filmmaking is also very important. Mother says our land inspires people to write about what they see and to express how they feel. And now we are free to tell our stories.

Mother encourages us to do what we love to do, with feeling. She calls it passion. It is the way she feels about her work as a doctor and caring for us. I feel that way about my schoolwork. At least I study very hard. When I am older, maybe I will study medicine like my mother, or find cures for diseases, or maybe be a scientist and live in a space station. In the pictures taken of our planet from

space, the world looks so peaceful. I wish it was! Maybe countries should settle their differences through sports, or in a big chess tournament.

Our countries had a race to space that seemed like good competition to me. We put the first spacecraft, *Sputnik I,* into orbit, and Yuri Gagarin was the first man in space. Space scientists from both our countries have made very big accomplishments. An American science team worked with Russian scientists to send a spacecraft to Mars. Then there was the Russian cosmonaut who went on the *Discovery* space shuttle to practice the rendezvous with our *Mir* space station. Your astronaut said, "We are bringing our nations closer together and into the next millennium!" It is a great start, this partnership in space.

President Mikhail Gorbachev and President Ronald Reagan worked to stop our governments from collecting nuclear weapons and to end the Cold War. Before that, people only saw the differences in our governments instead of the similarities of the people. I hope that the fear and distrust between our countries will be replaced with cooperation and lasting peace.

With "perestroika," you are welcome to visit here. We can talk to strangers on the bus, or be pen pals like us. People all over Russia are meeting tourists from foreign lands and making new friends. Our billboards advertise Apple Computers and Coca Cola. We have McDonald's hamburgers and 31 Flavors ice cream! We have televisions, computers, and fax machines that bring the outside world to us. Life may not be easy, but now we can communicate. I am writing this on a Macintosh at school. Babushka says that friendship comes from hearts reaching out and finding others reaching back. From my heart, I send you a big bear hug and three kisses on the cheek. That is our custom.

Do svidaniia. Good-bye.
From your new friend,

Elina

the netherlands

Dear Pen Pal,

Goed dag. My name is Meike. I am Dutch and live on a farm north of Amsterdam, in the Netherlands. Netherlands means "low country." You may also know my country as Holland. In my country there are no mountains, but there are over 3,000 kilometers of rivers, and almost half the land is below the level of the sea. Now you know why we wear "klompen"(wooden shoes)—to keep our feet dry!

You might say that the ocean is our worst enemy. The sand dunes are all that keep the powerful sea from flooding our land. The Dutch people have strengthened these dunes and replaced sections worn out by the sea with strong walls called "dykes." The dykes are always checked for holes or leaks. We have a saying here: "God created the world, but the Dutch made the Netherlands!" Dutch people actually drained water from the wetlands to make "polders" (fields). Polders are areas surrounded by dykes that have had the water pumped out. This was first done using windmills, but now we have steam and electric pumps. You can see windmills all over the Netherlands still, but they are mostly used to generate electricity.

The dykes were strong during the big flood of 1995. But my grandfather told me about the 1953 flood, when the storm was too big and the dykes gave way. His farm was flooded and lost, villages were ruined, and hundreds of people and farm animals drowned. But my grandfather, and the other brave people, helped to pump the water out and take back their land from the sea. In my history class, I learned that the dykes have also helped defend us from invading armies. You see, by opening up the dykes and flooding our enemy, we have won some battles! Can you imagine an army floating away to sea? Another time, the canals were frozen and we won by fighting on ice skates!

Most of us are good ice skaters. We get lots of practice because our winters are very long and cold. When winter is cold enough to freeze the canals, we have the Eleven Towns Race. At the last race, my older brother, Karl, got a trophy just for finishing! There are prizes for the fastest skaters but also for anyone strong enough to finish, because it is very difficult to do. The course is 50 kilometers long!

Most Dutch people also ride bicycles. Our land is so flat, it is quite easy. When the wind blows at our backs, we don't even have to pedal! Children ride to school, and men and women ride to work. In fact, my great-great-grandmother opened the first bicycle shop in den Hague, our capital. Even Queen Beatrix and the royal family are seen riding their bicycles. And I have seen Dutch military band members play instruments while pedaling their bicycles in formation!

Our family raises cows. One of my chores is to help with the milking. Lucky me! We sell the milk to factories, where it is made into powdered milk, or cheese (like Edam and Gouda), or milk chocolate. I adore chocolate! I think Dutch chocolate is the best in the world. I am sending you some to get your opinion! Neighboring farms grow grain, potatoes, and flower bulbs that are sold to other countries.

My father says our whole country has suffered from "tulipmania" ever since tulips were brought here from Turkey. Every house has tulips in pots or in gardens. The Netherlands has many beautiful gardens on large estates. Some are old castles with turrets and towers. In May, Mother took me to the Keukenhof, near Lisse, to celebrate the 400-year anniversary of the tulip! These gardens are open to the public for only a few weeks each spring to show off the 6 million bulbs in bloom. We saw a parade with garden floats and we went into the hothouses, where the most rare and fragile blossoms are grown. I grow lots of tulips in our garden. To me, they are like a quilt of color that covers the land.

Madurodam, near the Hague, is another place that I think you would enjoy. This tiny city has a town council, including a mayor, made up of Dutch children from the Hague. It is really just a park. There you can see our entire country in miniature! There are famous buildings and churches, a polder, an airport, and a city. Tiny people, trains, and cars move around, and ships sail in the small canals.

Next week Karl is taking me with him to Amsterdam. He has tickets to see the Ajax, Amsterdam's professional "voetbal" (soccer) team. I love going to Amsterdam and staying with our Aunt Nelleke. Amsterdam is our largest city, our "hoofdstad," or head city. It is built along canals, and there are a thousand bridges. At night they are lit with hundreds of lights! On the Singel Canal, there is a floating flower market that is over 100 years old. There are also stalls along the canals where we always buy raw herring, smoked salmon and eel, or other fish, like bass or turbot. For a special treat, we get apple tarts covered in cinnamon! On my last trip, Aunt Nelleke and I went to Delft to buy a piece of Delftware, the beautiful blue-and-white china we are known for. Delft is near the Hague, not far from Amsterdam. We found the piece we wanted at the De Porceleyne Fles factory, the original manufacturer of Delftware. I saw how the china is hand-painted the same way it has been for 300 years. I sent you a small tile. Did it arrive in one piece?

Along the canals, there are tall houses with gabled roofs. Many were built by wealthy merchants who made their fortunes buying and selling products, like spices and diamonds, from around the world. Diamond cutting is still an important business here. You can tell by all the jewelry stores! The funniest house in Amsterdam, I think, is

#7 Singel. It is very narrow, just a little wider than your arms stretched out! The story goes that a merchant had it built for his coachman, who had once said that he would be happy with a house as wide as his master's front door, and that is exactly what he got. Always remember, if you ask for something, you just might get it.

Sometimes we take the museum boat, which stops at many museums along the canal, like the Rijksmuseum and the Van Gogh National Museum. Amsterdam has so many art museums because it has been a center of painting since the Middle Ages. I saw Rembrandt's collection of etchings and prints at his house. It is now a museum, but it is the same as it was when he lived there in the 17th century. With your interest in angels, you would probably enjoy Rembrandt's engraving, *Angel Appearing to the Shepherds*. Do you think angels really watch over us? I read a book of recent stories about people who said that they were led to safety, or taken out of danger, by an angel, or someone, who disappeared as quickly as he appeared. I like to think that angels are close by to help us. Maybe all we need to do is ask for help when we are in trouble? I think if angels could appear to the shepherds in the Bible, then they can appear to us too.

There is one house in Amsterdam that touches me the most, the Anne Frank House. Have you read *The Diary of Anne Frank?* This is the house where Anne and her family hid from the Nazis for two years during World War II. I looked at her small wooden desk in her room, where 50 years ago she wrote her diary. In a different way than Samantha Smith, this young girl made a difference, at least to me. Now, I cannot forget Anne, her family, and the millions of others who died during the war. That desk reminds me that we need to make our world a better place. A place of love, not hate, so that something like this will never happen again.

In the Netherlands, we respect the power of the sea. I know the damage that a little drop of water can cause. It may seem to be only one little drop, but when it is one of many, many little drops, they become an ocean with enormous power! If people everywhere respect and trust each other, then we can find great strength and peace. Then, just as the drop of water joins others to become an ocean, together we can be like the ripples you spoke of, spreading and spreading, becoming stronger and more powerful, until we fill the whole world with love. Then there would be no walls or dykes to keep us back!

Vele Groetjes. Your Dutch Pen Pal,

Meike

saudi arabia

Dear Pen Pal,

Marhaba. Hello. My name is Khalid, and I live with my family in the city of Riyadh in Saudi Arabia. Saudi Arabia covers most of the Arabian Peninsula, the land between Africa and Asia. You might not know very much about my country or my people. Do you picture us living in tents, wandering the vast deserts? The bedouin people are still nomads like this, but most Saudis live in cities, as you do in America.

Riyadh means "gardens" in Arabic. It was built on an oasis. An oasis is a fertile area in the desert, where there are underground springs that supply water. Riyadh is our royal capital. Well over a million people live here. We have high-rise office blocks, traffic jams, eight-lane highways, and the largest airport in the world. My family lives in a tower-block apartment. My sisters Huda and Laila share a room and I have my own!

Sometimes I wear western clothes, but most men wear "thobes," the long white robes like the one I am wearing in my picture. They are cooler in the desert heat. The "keffiyeh" (headdresses) we wear also provide shade. In the summer, it can be hotter than 49 degrees centigrade (in Fahrenheit, that is 120 degrees!). Mother wears western clothes at home, but when she goes out she always covers her head and wears her "abbaya," a black silky cloak. We shop in the "souks," our traditional markets, in the evenings, when it is cooler. Our newer shopping centers are indoors and air-conditioned, so we can shop there any time of day.

I have tasted many different foods at foreign restaurants here, but I like what Mother cooks the best! Usually, she roasts chicken, lamb, or goat (we never eat pork because of our religion), and it is served on a big platter of spicy rice. We eat lots of vegetables, fruit, almonds, and dates, which are grown here. I also like yogurt and falafel. Falafel are a spicy mixture of ground garbanzo beans made into patties that are fried, then stuffed along with lettuce, tomatoes, and hot sauce into pita bread (flat, round pocket bread). Everyone drinks coffee here. Our family serves coffee with great ritual and ceremony. First, we roast the beans, then we grind them, and then the beans are boiled with cardamom seeds and sugar. It is served in little cups. If you visited us, you would see that we always eat or drink with family or friends. To us, eating is a social event. We share stories of our day and the latest news over meals. My father says that this time is important for our family's togetherness and friendship.

My father is the manager of a desalinization plant. They take salt out of seawater to make it fresh for drinking. This is very important for a country with so little water. When I am older, I want to take environmental studies at King Faud University to learn how to take care of the earth! Father says we need to look for other energy solutions and develop industries not related to oil, because the earth only has so much!

Before the discovery of oil, our country had changed very little since Biblical times. Riyadh was once a mud-walled village, and our country was divided among many warring groups. In 1902, Ibn Saud, a young prince, united them. He became King of Saudi Arabia in 1932. That same year, an American oil company discovered "black gold"—oil! This discovery, near Hasa along the coast, made Saud's poor kingdom one of the richest in the world! The oil industry has provided jobs for many Saudis and for many foreigners too. The construction business also grew. Now we have new factories, refineries, houses, schools and universities, hospitals, roads, seaports and airports. I also have more opportunities to have a life I really want.

Near the border of Iraq is the Nafud Desert. This is the land of the bedouin nomads, the wanderers who, even today, live in tents. The Nafud gets enough rain to provide grass for the sheep, goats, and camels to eat. Many stories have been passed down about life in the desert. The bedouins were as hard as the desert they lived on. Survival was most important. They took care of their family first, then their tribe. The "sheiks," or old men, were their leaders. And to them, dignity was sacred. They believed in the saying, "An eye for an eye." But they were also known for their hospitality. If a stranger, even an enemy, kissed or touched the hem of a bedouin's tent, they were guaranteed three days of hospitality! The bedouins knew if you refused food, water, or shelter to anyone in the desert, it would mean death. The bedouins supplied camels to caravans for thousands of years. At one time, a man's wealth was counted by how many camels he owned. Now, it is how many barrels of oil you have! Today, many bedouins have traded camels for cars and moved into cities to work. It is probably an easier life. Besides, camels are not air-conditioned, and the ones I have known are quite nasty. They kick, bite, spit, and even whine when you put a load on their back.

Saudis love to tell stories. You may know some of our most famous tales, such as "Ali Baba and the Forty Thieves," or "Sheherezade," or (I know you know this one) "Aladdin." They come from the legends told in the *Arabian Nights*. My parents read me these stories when I was little, and I still enjoy them. We also read the Qur'an, or Koran. It is our sacred book. We believe the Koran to be the actual words of God that were revealed to Muhammed and written down by his secretary (Muhammed couldn't read or write, you see). It is also believed that the angel Jibril (Gabriel to you) came to Muhammed and told him he would be the last prophet of Allah, or God. (You see, we do believe in angels!) Gabriel is the same angel that came to Moses. He was a prophet before Muhammed. We believe there were many prophets before Muhammed: Adam, Noah, Abraham, Moses, Jesus, and Buddha were some of the most important ones.

It would be hard for you to understand my people without knowing about the Islamic faith, because our history, culture, and laws are rooted in Islamic beliefs. These are based

on the Koran and the Old Testament of the Bible. Islam means "commitment to Allah." People who make that commitment are Muslims. Our lives revolve around our faith. There are five things, called the Five Pillars, a Muslim does to be a good Muslim. They are: shahada, salat, zakat, sawn, and hajj.

"Shahada" is when you profess your faith in Allah. "Salat" is praying five times a day. Wherever I am, I stop, put down my prayer rug (I always have it with me), face Mecca, and pray. "Zakat" means we give what we can to the poor. During the month of Ramadan, an important holiday, we fast; this is "sawn." We do not eat or drink anything while there is daylight, and believe me, it is very hard to do! And finally, there is "hajj." Someday, I will make a hajj, or pilgrimage, to al-Haram, the Great Mosque in Mecca. It can hold 300,000 people at one time! This is the most sacred shrine of Islam. I will be one of the millions of Muslims who come from all over the world to Mecca. We will walk around the Ka'aba, the black stone in the center of the mosque, and pray. All Muslims make this special journey to Mecca at least once during their lifetimes. Over the years, many followers, from many different lands, have come to Mecca. By exchanging ideas, they have helped unify and strengthen the empire of Islam.

Over the years, Muslims have also exchanged knowledge. Did you know that the numbers you use are from the Hindu-Arabic numeral system? This system created the number zero. It comes from the Arabic word that means "empty." Without zero, you could not even have some numbers!

The modern influence in our country has come from foreign people, and their ideas and products. Some people here are afraid we might lose our Arabic identity. Perhaps that is why we are careful to maintain our own identity. It is the ancient and the new, living side by side. But if we try to respect each other's beliefs, we can live side by side.

I think that instead of summit meetings, people from different countries should have a feast together. Then, while the children play, the families (or countries) can get to know one another. There would be no quarreling. Some would prefer bread, and others rice, so each would eat what they preferred. I think, as with food, the human mind likes different flavors, and that is why there is a variety of religions. At this feast, even though we would speak different languages, dress differently, or have different beliefs, we could learn to honor each other and have peace in our lives. Perhaps, someday, you will come to my country and we can go on a picnic together.

Maa Alsalama Good-bye,

Khalid

canada

Dear Pen Pal,

Hello. My name is Joshua. Call me Josh, everyone does. I'm Canadian. We live near the city of Calgary, in the province of Alberta. There are 10 provinces (like your 50 states) in Canada, and two territories. We are one of the biggest countries in the world, but there are only as many people here as you have in California.

Most Canadians live in the south, along the U.S. border, because it's the warmest part. Trappers and fishermen live in the Northwest Territories and the Yukon, where there are snow-covered mountains and forests and it's very cold. The only people who live very far north, in the Canadian Arctic, are the Inuit, which means "real people." We sometimes call them Eskimos, like you do. It is believed that the Inuit came here from Asia 5,000 years ago. Why do you think they settled here, where it's so cold, and not further south? Even the birds fly south!

Did you know there isn't any land under the North Pole? It's an ocean, a sea of ice! I'd always heard that Eskimos lived in "igloos," houses made of ice. So when I went there with my dad on a trip, I was surprised because I didn't see any igloos! Now, most Eskimos live in houses. They fish from motorboats instead of "kayaks" and ride snowmobiles! I did see a dogsled race, but sleds are used mostly for sport now. Supposedly, there are remote areas of the Arctic where the Eskimos still live as they always did. Did you know that Eskimos believe that every child has a guardian spirit? Another angel for your collection, eh?

The very first Canadians were the Inuit and our native people (you call them Native Americans). They say our name, Canada, comes from the Huron-Iroquois word "kanata," which means village or community. The Indians that live along the Pacific Coast are famous for their fine wood carving. They carve wonderful ceremonial masks. When we lived in British Columbia, I saw some of their totem poles. They don't make totem poles anymore, but you can see them in museums. The Glenbow Museum has a great Indian collection. The carvings on totem poles show a picture history of events that happen in a family. What would you carve to show your family's history?

British Columbia is beautiful. Most of the land and tall mountains there are covered with thick forests. I have watched logs being towed downstream to the mills. Logging is the major industry in that area, and much of the wood is made into paper for newspapers. My best memories of going there are fishing. That's where my dad taught me fly-fishing for river trout and where I caught a 25-pound king salmon by myself! (I sent a picture to prove it!) I loved living near all the forest

animals: beavers, elk, moose, foxes, squirrels, and chipmunks. One day, my brother Matt and I saw two cuddly bear cubs in the forest behind our cabin. Without thinking, we started toward them. Suddenly, we heard a loud roar! We didn't know where their mother was, but she was too close for us. We ran away so fast! We learned a good lesson—we should respect our neighbours the bears, and enjoy them from a distance! I think I would carve a fish and a bear on my totem pole.

I have some Blackfoot Indian ancestry on my mother's side of the family. They lived and hunted buffalo right here on the plain where our city was built. European hunters and trappers came in the 1600s. Canada was called New France for a while, and then it became a British colony. Western Canada wasn't developed until gold was discovered in the Yukon Territory. The gold rush brought many more settlers from Europe. My dad's grandparents came here from Scotland. Our city was named for Calgary in Scotland. In Gaelic, Calgary means "clear, running water." Fort Calgary was actually built for the North West Mounted Police. Do you know why the Mounties wear red jackets? The Indians considered red a symbol of justice and fair dealings. They had respected the British soldiers who came to the west before the Mounties, and who wore red coats!

My dad is in the Royal Canadian Mounted Police. That's our national police force. In the movies, the Mounties are always the guys who track criminals over snow and ice in Canada's forests and wilderness, never stopping until they get their man! They are still called Mounties even though they don't always ride horses like they used to. Dad rides in a car, or a snowmobile, or sometimes a plane when they have to patrol the territories. But he does ride his horse during ceremonies and parades. I think my father is a good example of the Mounties' motto: To Maintain the Law. He insists that we always tell the truth, even when it seems easier not to. My parents have also taught us to do what we believe is right, and to speak out when we feel something is wrong. Dad says if we live like this, whether or not we become rich or famous, we will be successful in whatever we choose to do!

When I was young I wanted to be a Mountie like my dad. Then I wanted to be a professional cowboy. We have horses on our ranch. Matt and I have been riding since before we could walk! (More pictures!) Calgary might be considered an oil town now, but it started as a cattle town. There are many ranches here. Every July we go to the annual Calgary Exhibition and Stampede, The World's Largest Rodeo! After the free breakfast of flapjacks and bacon, and after the square dancers have whooped it up in the streets, we go see the famous chuck-wagon race and the horse races. To me, the most exciting part is the rodeo events. I love to watch the bucking-brahma-bull riding and the calf roping, where cowboys race against the clock to stay on the bull or get the calf down! Now that I am older and wiser, I'm thinking about being a forest ranger. I love being outside, and it's probably safer than being a cowboy.

Since Calgary is in the foothills of the Rocky Mountains, we go skiing, snowshoe-ing, and tobogganing most of the winter. I play in an ice hockey league, similar to your baseball leagues. I'm the goalie. I guard the net, so I need to wear a face mask and lots of padding! In the warmer months, my friends and I also play base-ball, soccer, and football. But ice hockey is our national sport (go Calgary Flames!). Lacrosse was our first sport. Our native people played it. Lacrosse is similar to ice hockey, but it is played on a grass field, without skates. You use long sticks with little baskets on the ends to catch and throw the ball. You don't need to wear pads, but you wear a lot of black eyes!

A couple of summers ago, we took a family trip east. We drove and camped across Canada, to Quebec and back! We drove through the three Prairie Provinces, Saskatchewan, Manitoba, and Ontario, and saw why they're sometimes called the "food basket of the world." Crops grow as far as you can see. In Ontario, we drove along the largest freshwater lakes in the world, the Great Lakes. We share them with your country. Niagara Falls are on the border between Ontario and New York. Did you see them on your trip? I thought the waterfalls were amazing! We also went to Quebec City, Canada's oldest city. It was once a French colony, so many of the people there have kept their French culture and language. Stop signs in Quebec City say, Arret! Many Canadian products have French labels too, because both French and English are our national languages.

Last year we took a camping trip south, following the Trail of the Great Bear. This trail links our two countries and celebrates the gift of national parks, which let everyone enjoy the natural beauty of the land. We saw glacial ice fields at Banff and Jasper, Canada's first national parks. Then we went to Wyoming and watched the geyser, Old Faithful, blow its top at Yellowstone National Park. (Maybe you already know that Yellowstone was the very first national park anywhere in the entire world!) We also stopped at Indian sites and museums, like you did on your trip. I think I learned a lot about the native people who lived at the different places we stopped. On the way home, we camped at Waterton Glacier Park. Our countries share this park. It has been named the world's first International Peace Park and is a symbol of friendship between your country and mine. Maybe nature knows no boundaries, at least not like people do.

I really enjoy being outside in nature. Like you at the beach, it makes me feel peaceful. My mom says nature is "food for the soul." Native people believe the earth is sacred and that harming it not only hurts us, but shows disrespect to the creator. They worry about the forests being used up and about animals, like the grizzly bear and the eagle, fading away like the buffalo did. At school we read a letter that Chief Seattle wrote to the U.S. president in 1850. He wrote:

> We are part of the earth and it is part of us…The white man must treat the beasts of this land as his brothers…For whatever happens to the beasts, soon happens to man. All things are connected…Teach your children what we have taught our children, that the earth is our mother…Preserve the land for all children and love it…We are brothers after all.

I think that people who live close to nature feel connected to everything, like we are all a part of each other. The Blackfoot Indian word "kunaitupii" means "all the people," and to me that means we are all related to each other.

Best Regards. Your Friend,

Joshua

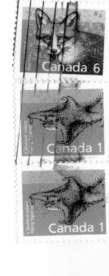

germany

Dear Pen Pal,

Guten tag. Hello. My name is Hans. I live in Germany, which is in the center of Europe. The Baltic Sea and North Sea are to our north, and the Alps are to the south. When I was born, my country was called West Germany, or the Federal Republic of Germany. East Germany was another country. Now there is one united Germany. We are no longer divided into east and west.

My family lives in a large brick house near the city of Köln; you may know it as Cologne. The Rhine River is like a water highway that runs through Köln. It is the longest river in western Europe and carries the most cargo of any river in all of Europe. The hillsides along the Rhine are terraced to grow grapes for some of the best wine in the world. If you traveled on the Rhine, you would see cities with castle ruins and fortresses that are hundreds of years old. I have been through many of these castles. The stone makes them very cold, and they are just a bit spooky. They really do look like the castles in the fairy tales you read as a child. I am sure you have read some of the folktales from my country. "Snow White," "Hansel and Gretl," and "Sleeping Beauty" are some of my favorites that were written by the Grimm brothers, who were German.

Do you have festivals in your country? I love our "fests." They are always fun; the whole town celebrates. And the food is "wunderbar"! I love to eat wiener wurstchen, the cousins of your hot dogs, and bratwurst, a kind of sausage. My favorite dessert is schwarzwalderkirschtorte. This is a very long word for Black Forest cake, a chocolate cake with cherries! My favorite fest is Karneval. It actually starts in the 11th month, on the 11th day, at the 11th hour and second, when Hopeditz, the spirit of the season, awakens. This is a very long fest, lasting all winter. The Monday before Aschen Mittwoch (Ash Wednesday) is called Rosen Montag. On this day, the wildest festivities take place. There are huge parades (like your Rose Bowl Parade) with floats and bands, jesters, and a king and queen. I think it is also similar to your Mardi Gras in New Orleans, because candy and goodies are thrown from the floats. This year, I tried holding an umbrella upside down to catch as much candy as possible. It worked very well! Another wonderful fest is at the end of summer. It is the Rhein in Flammen, or the Rhine in Flames. All the towns and castles along the Rhine are lit up with colored lights. There are bonfires and fireworks all up and down the river. It looks magical!

We also celebrate trick or treat, but a little differently than you do. In our version, trick or treat begins when St. Martin rides to our school at the end

of the day wearing a red coat and black boots (sounds a little familiar?). All the children make lanterns that we carry as we follow St. Martin through town. (My parents used to put candles in their lanterns. Today things are more high-tech—we use flashlights!) After walking through our neighborhood singing loudly, we go trick-or-treating. At each house, we must sing to get our treats. I learned when I was very young that I did more damage than good by singing, so now I stand quietly at the back and present my bag at just the right moment.

My grandparents live outside Munich, in a wooden châlet at the foot of the Bavarian Alps. Munich is known for other things besides its famous beer. It is also an important industrial and cultural center, with many museums. The last time we visited my grandparents, they took us to Nymphenburg Palace (Castle of the Nymphs) to see the royal family's summer residence. It is very old and beautiful, and has a wonderful park with four garden buildings. One of them, called Badenburg, has a very grand indoor swimming pool! My grandmother told me that more than half of her beautiful city was destroyed during World War II. The royal palace was badly damaged and so was the Frauenkirche, the Church of our Lady, which has since been restored. Our famous cathedral in Köln was not destroyed. Can you imagine, it took over 600 years to build it!

The German people have a long tradition of hand craftsmanship, such as wood carving and making toys, cuckoo clocks, and musical instruments. My grandpa loves to carve and make things with his hands. Every Christmas, Grandpa makes us something special. My most special gift was the cuckoo clock he made me the year I learned to tell time! I sent you a little one to remind you of your German pen pal, me!

Christmas in my country is very beautiful. There are lights everywhere and snow on all the buildings and trees! Did you know that Germany started the custom of Christmas trees? Trees are usually decorated by the father and children while the mother bakes cookies. These are placed under the tree with presents from the Christ Child, or Christ Kind. You see, in Germany, St. Nikolaus comes several weeks before Christmas. You enter the living room with your mother to find St. Nikolaus waiting, dressed in his red coat, white beard, and black boots. He is holding a large book and a bundle of branches (I think you call them switches). He keeps an exact record of each child's activities for the whole year! He knows if you have been bad or good. If you are good, you get presents! If you are not, well, he is holding those branches

for a reason. During Christmastime, the outdoor Christmas bazaars sell anything you want, from ornaments and folk art to toys and delicious treats like gingerbread, sausages, and roasted chestnuts. These Christmas markets date back to medieval times. The one in Munich is the oldest. It is 600 years old. And, you will like this, in Augsburg, they have "living Christmas angels" who sing from the windows in the town. They are really just people in costume, but it is still a sight to see!

My country is known for classical music. Maybe because many famous composers were German, like Bach, Beethoven, Mozart, Handel, Brahms, and Strauss, just to name a few. My sister Marta is eight and she takes piano lessons. I told her that she might as well give up because she is already too old! Mozart started playing when he was three and had written his first symphony when he was eight. Beethoven was four when he started and was on tour by age 11! Mother tells her not to listen to me and to play because she enjoys it. I know that, but she is my little sister, after all.

I think it is an exciting time to be alive. It certainly has been in Germany. There have been so many changes. For hundreds of years before the world wars, Germany was a very great nation, but after the second war, Germany was divided into two countries. West Germany was a democracy, and East Germany was a communist country. Berlin, our capital, was also divided into east and west zones. People who were unhappy in East Germany crossed into West Germany through Berlin. To stop this, the East German government built a concrete wall right in the middle of the city. The Berlin Wall was heavily guarded, and some people died trying leave East Germany. Imagine it, one day in 1961 you could go to school or visit friends and family in either country, and then, the next day, there is a big wall and you cannot get to the other side! In my mother's family, her aunt, uncle, and cousins lived on the other side, in East Germany. After the wall, they could no longer visit my mother and grandparents. This made everyone in my family very sad. I guess you really understand the meaning of freedom, when you no longer have it!

Once I asked my parents, "If the communist way of life is so good, why did they have to build a wall to keep people there?" I could never understand that. But now, 30 years later, the wall finally came down. I will never forget

that day, 9 November 1989. We watched people on television who were standing on the wall, chipping away at it, helping to tear it down. There was such noise and celebration in the streets after they broke through the wall. People could pass from east to west and from west to east! When my family was finally able to see their relatives again, we all cried. Marta and I met cousins we never knew, and we no longer wondered what was on the other side of the wall.

Manufacturing cars is an important business in Germany, with automobile companies like Volkswagen, BMW, Porsche, and Mercedes-Benz. My father is an engineer with Volkswagen, and he loves his job. He is very proud of the German reputation for building quality cars and other manufactured products. I would like very much to design cars someday. My father says I should do what I love, because then it will not seem like work at all!

What do I think about peace? I hope there is never another war. I know how hard the Germans have worked to rebuild their cities after the last one. We have learned much about facing difficulties from our past, and I think we are a stronger people now. The lessons of Hitler's inhumanity has taught us the importance of freedom for all and reminds us to love one another. We should never build walls again. Instead, we should build bridges to bring people together. Everyone should work as one big family to solve problems peacefully and create a brotherhood of nations!

Auf wiedersehen. Good-bye from your new freund,

Hans

india

Dear Pen Pal,

Nameste. Hello. My name is Deepa. I live in Bombay, the largest city in India. It is called the Gateway to India. Did you know that your Native Americans, or Indians, were named after us? Christopher Columbus was looking for an easy route to India, but he discovered America instead. Thinking he'd arrived in the Indies, he named the people he met there Indians! Bombay has always been an important port city. For centuries, explorers and merchants have come here to buy jewels, silks, rugs, and spices from the Orient.

My father is a merchant. He sells many products in his store that have been made in India, but mostly clothing. Our family lives in a flat above my father's store. My older sister and brother are both married. My brother Sanjay, his wife, Asha, and their little boy live with us. So, I am an aunt! My nephew, Ram, has big brown eyes and is usually very good. When I'm not in school, I help take care of him. My sister Parvati lives with her husband, Arun, and his family on a farm outside Bombay. In many Indian families, a girl's parents find her a suitable husband when she is old enough to get married. But I want to go to university, so I do not think this will happen. It is very expensive to go, and I must work very hard. I will try to get a scholarship. I do not know what I will study yet. Maybe I will become a teacher and help educate the children of India. Or perhaps I can make wonderful films. Now, that would be the dream of 10 lifetimes!

I love going to the cinema. Did you know that more films are made in India than in any other country? The biggest studios are here in Bombay. You could call it the Hollywood of India! The Taj Mahal is the most photographed building in India. It is considered one of the most beautiful buildings in the world! It was built in the 1600s by a Moslem ruler as a tomb for Arjumad Banu Began. She was also known as Mumtaz Mahal, which means Crown of the Palace. The building is all white marble! The Moslem ruler wanted it to be as beautiful as she was. Isn't that romantic? They say it took 20,000 workers and 20 years to complete!

Sometimes, Father takes me to the fabric mills and other places he goes to buy the things he sells in his store. I like to watch the fabric painters cover the carved wooden blocks with paint and press them into the fabric. Bombay is the leading Indian city for weavers of cotton, and we export

the fabric all over the world. Not everyone who works in the textile industry works in the mills. I have visited cottage industries and watched the weavers make fine fabrics or beautiful rugs in their homes. One woman gave me some lace I had watched her make from silver and golden threads. I can't wait until Mother sews it on my favourite "salwar-kammez," a traditional dress girls and women wear.

My family practices Hinduism. It is a religion, but it is also a way of life. We have many sacred writings like the Vedas, our oldest scriptures, and the Mahabharata, which is a book of tales about five princes who tried to get their kingdom back and the struggles they faced along the way. In Hindu, specific trades are called "jati." Most relatives have the same jati, such as barbers, merchants, or carpenters. Professionals, like doctors, are said to work outside of the jati. Since our family jati is "vaishya," the merchant, Sanjay works with my father to learn the business. Our famous leader Gandhi, who was known as Mahatma ("Great Soul"), was also vaishya. But he went on to university in England and became a lawyer, which was outside the jati. He was very important in helping India to become an independent nation. He believed in peaceful and nonviolent resistance, which he called Satyagraha, or "holding fast to the truth."

Much of my city looks like western cities I have seen in movies, with lots of people, houses, apartments, and skyscrapers. Most of the architecture here is British, because we were once a British colony. The British East Indian Trading Company built railroads and roads all over the country.

I have fun visiting my sister and her family on their farm. I miss her very much and am always happy to see her. I don't mind helping her with the chores. I like to feed the animals, especially the cows. Cows are sacred to Hindus, and are a symbol of the Mother Goddess. We would never kill them, so we never eat beef! They are also useful because they pull carts and plows, and give us milk to make butter and cheese. After visiting the farm, I am always happy to come home and go back to school. In some parts of India, going to school after you are 11 years old is a privilege. Some children do not continue their schooling but instead learn the craft of their fathers. They work in factories or on family farms, like the children who work with my sister. My sister says many farmers are needed because our population grows so fast. We already have over 800 million people in India! Feeding all of us is a big task!

Farmers depend on the monsoons. The monsoon is "the season of the rains," from June to September. At the harvest festival we celebrate the coming of the monsoon. If we don't get enough rain, the crops will not grow. If the rains come too late, or if there is flooding, the crops can be ruined. Rain turns to snow on the Himalayan Mountains and the snow melts into the many rivers, like the Ganges, that flow and bring life to the earth. This makes the ground fertile to grow the food to feed our people. That is why we celebrate the rain. Rain is the bringer of life.

The highest mountain in the world, Mount Everest, is in our Himalayas. It is 8,872 meters tall and stands in our Greater Himalayan Mountains. This mountain range separates India from Tibet and China. Himalaya means "home of the snow." I have seen movies about explorers who have tried to climb Mount Everest. It is like a giant that looks over the tiny country of Tibet. Buddhist monks and priests have lived in stone monasteries high in the Himalayas for centuries. They passed down from Buddha, from teacher to pupil, the spiritual art of making sand mandalas (I've sent a photo). Mandalas are circular designs that symbolize parts of the universe. In his store, my father has mandalas made of coloured sand, of stones and rice, of flowers, and some are even made of jewels. Father told me that each colour and design shows the oneness of things and has a special meaning, like compassion or wisdom.

On the southern slopes of the Lesser Himalayas is the "jangal" (jungle), with monkeys, tigers, snakes, elephants, and all the animals that Rudyard Kipling wrote about. He wrote *The Jungle Book*. Kipling was an Englishman, but he was born in India and lived here most of his life. I have not been to the jungle, but Kipling makes me feel that I have. In one *Jungle Book* story, Mowgli the boy-cub was raised by wolves. His friends, Bagheera the panther and Baloo the bear, protect him from the fierce tiger, Shere Khan, and help him survive in the jungle. It is still one of my favourite books. And now Ram loves it too. He wants me to read it to him over and over again.

The Barapuv National Park used to be a hunting reserve for the Maharajas. Today, it is a very important ecological park where you can see tigers, bears, and rhinoceroses. At the park all the animals native to India are protected. I have never seen a tiger, but monkeys and elephants are as common to us as the deer in your backyard. This is the land of the elephant! Every village in India has its own temple elephant. The ancient

temples had them carved in stone. Elephants are brought into the marketplaces and decorated during ceremonies. I have heard of white elephants, but they are very rare. They were considered omens of good fortune and were kept by kings. I guess it is easy to tame elephants. They work with people hauling logs in the forests and are also used for transportation. The Indian elephants are the kind you see in circuses. They are smaller than African elephants, I think.

In India, we have an old story. Six blind men were each trying to explain an elephant. The first man describes its trunk; the second, its tail; the third, its tusk; the next, a leg; another, its smell; and the last, the sound it made. Each description was so different, yet they were all explaining the same animal! Our "gurus" (teachers) say that this is the same as each person experiencing Brahma, or God. Each person experiences Him in his or her own way.

I believe the prophets and gods of all religions are just different faces of Brahma. As a Hindu, I also believe that during our life on earth we learn lessons of peace, harmony, and brotherhood and that we come back each lifetime to see if we have learned a lesson from the past. We are each responsible for our own thoughts, words, and deeds. If we hurt someone, we hurt ourselves, and what we give out, we get back. This is what we call "karma." True peace comes from within each of us. Gandhi called it the "little voice within." When personal peace is found, our inner lights will light the world. Then it will be possible for nations to get along. Remember this old Hindu saying, "The world is as we are."

Nameste. Goodbye. (We use the same word to greet you as we do to wish you farewell.) This word also means, "I celebrate the place in you where we are both one."

Your Pen Pal,

Deepa

china

Dear Pen Pal,

Ni how. Hello! I am Lee Ying. My home is Shanghai, on the east coast of Asia, in the People's Republic of China. I have read that a quarter of the world's population lives in China and that there are more Chinese in the world than any other people. Over a billion people just in China! Shanghai is a very busy and crowded city on the Yangtze River. Most of China's cargo is shipped through this port. As I look around, it is hard to believe that Shanghai was a small fishing village just 100 years ago. Now, Shanghai, which means "up from the sea," is Asia's biggest city.

My older brother, two younger sisters, and I live with my parents and my grand-parents in an apartment above the market that my father owns. His father owned it before him. My brother, Lee Wu, and I help in the market when we are not in school, because someday the market will be passed to us. Sometimes I go with him to the docks where he buys fish. At the docks, day or night, you can hear the sirens and horns of hundreds of boats passing by. There are barges and steamers, ferries with hundreds of passengers, and always the junks and sampans. "Junks" are sailboats with flat bottoms. Some Chinese people have used junks to live on and for trans-portation for thousands of years. I am sending you a picture of what they look like. "Sampans" are smaller boats that are moved with a single oar called a "yuloh." Thousands of Chinese families call them home. They can fish, sell their fish, buy things from other floating markets, and never have to leave the river.

How would I describe my city to you? The new section, along the river's edge, is much like photos I have seen of your cities. It has wide streets with modern sky-scrapers, department stores, and hotels, like our Peace Hotel, with its tall, green, pointed tower. In the mornings, along Nanjing Road, you see people of all ages in the parks. They practice musical instruments or singing, or do exercises called "tai-jichuan," or shadow boxing, before they go to work or school. The building where we live is in the older part of the city. Here, there are narrow streets with many markets, restaurants, and shops that sell anything you can imagine.

The people in my city dress more like you do, probably because our shopping area is more western style. We usually wear cotton for everyday, but our special clothing is made of silk. The Chinese were the first to raise silkworms for silk thread that is spun and woven into cloth. Do you have any silk clothes? I love to wear silk because it feels so soft and smooth.

Is it true that almost every American family has its own car? There are very few cars in China, but we have as many bicycles as there are people! That is how everyone here gets around. At one time, people were carried in small, two-wheeled carts called

"rickshaws" that were pulled by men. Now most rickshaws have been replaced by tricycle-taxis. We watch television. It is very popular in China. We see musical shows and news, which keeps us in touch across our huge country and now with the outside world too.

Most Chinese people love music and drama, juggling, magic and puppet shows, mimes, and dancing. Last month our family went to "jingxi" (or "ching-hsi"), the Beijing Opera, which is kind of an opera with words, singing, dancing, and acrobatics all in one. Each dancer must be an actor, singer, and acrobat. They use very specific hand movements designed just for the character they play. I would like very much to perform in the Beijing Opera when I am older. My singing might hold me back, though.

During the year, we have many festivals, such as the celebration of the New Year and the Dragon Boat Festival. Dragons are not scary to us. They are friendly and important creatures. I enjoy the traditional lion dance, where two men perform inside a lion costume, the parades, and, of course, firecrackers! Did you know the Chinese invented gunpowder?

We also love to eat and have great feasts. Each region of China has its own special foods and dishes. But most of the time our meals include grain, such as porridge, boiled rice, or noodles, that is served with vegetables, poultry, pork, fish, soya bean curd, and sauces. Mother cooks on top of the stove in a pan called a "wok." Our dinner usually ends with soup and fresh fruit. Do you know how to eat with chopsticks? We call them "kuaizi." We also drink lots of tea, which originally came from China. Tea helps digest your food.

Near the rivers the soil is very rich. That is where rice, our main food crop, is grown in fields called "paddies." Rice is grown in lowlands that can be flooded when needed. The rice plant is actually a type of long grass that grows from less than a meter to almost two meters tall. The part we eat is actually the seed. These fertile valleys are also home to the giant pandas. I have never seen one in the wild, only at the Xijiao Zoo, here in Shanghai. They may look like bears, but they are actually in the raccoon family. At the zoo, I also learned that over 400 different kinds of wild animals live in China, like the giant pandas in Szechwan, tigers in the northeast, elephants in Yunnan, and crocodiles in the Yangze river.

You wrote that you have a dog and a cat. I have goldfish, and my sister Lee Chu has a cricket she plans to take to the cricket races! It was interesting to hear that some of your cities have Chinatowns. I wonder if they are really like China. Perhaps someday you will come to visit us and I could show you my city. It is very nice to have a pen pal from the United States. At school we have studied about your country, but it is very different hearing about it from you. It is only recently that China has had contact with other countries in the world. My parents would not have been allowed to have pen pals. China is very large and isolated from everyone else. Our natural boundaries, the deserts and great mountains in the west, and the Pacific Ocean in the east, have kept us separate from other countries. There is

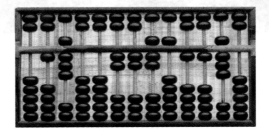

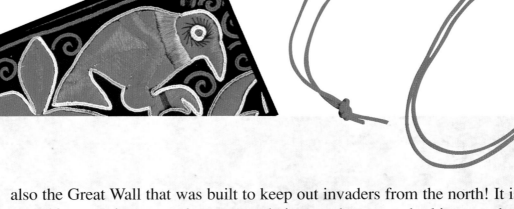

also the Great Wall that was built to keep out invaders from the north! It is quite magnificent. It is no wonder our people invented ways to do things on their own. Three thousand years ago, they were building cities, irrigating farms, making silk and paper, and writing picture symbols with a brush.

We still use that same written language. There are 8,000 characters that make up our language. People here do not ask children if we can read, but ask how many characters we know! These characters, we call them Hanzi, represent ideas, not sounds as in your alphabet. Now we are also learning a new phonetic alphabet called Pinyin that is based on the Latin alphabet. Someday it may replace our old characters. This will make it easier for us and other people to learn our language. This is another way our country is becoming part of the world community. Grandfather says the world seems to be getting smaller. I think it is good to learn more about the world outside our borders!

My grandfather has always taught us the sayings and beliefs of Confucius. He was a very wise teacher and philosopher in the sixth century. Confucius believed that there is goodness in the center of each of us and if you are your true self you would be good. He also taught people that they should be honest and kind, and honor their parents and elders. Confucius said, "Do not to others what you do not wish others to do to you." Grandfather says you have a very similar saying, called the Golden Rule. My family follows the wisdom of Confucius, but also we study the teachings of Buddha and Lao Tze, who writes about the Tao, which means "the way." Grandfather says these teachings make harmony with each other, and are different roads to the same end. He says different religions are like a feast on a banquet table. There are many foods to choose from and some people prefer meat, and others like vegetables. You simply take what you need to nourish you and leave the rest for others to use. I think if everyone did this, we could find a road to peace.

Best wishes to you and your family. Zaijian. Farewell,

Lee Ying

What a great project this has been! I have learned so much from my new pen pal friends. And it seems we are all interested in making the world a more peaceful place. All of us have our own dreams to fulfill: to become a doctor like Maria, or an artist like Gianni, design cars like Hans, or to be Andre, the Grand Chef de Cuisine. Some of us want to be athletes like Lee Ying who wants to be a gymnast. Josh wants to be outside and be a forest ranger. And some of us are musical or want to dance like Sarah Rebekah. Cameron and Juan want to be scientists and study archaeology or astronomy, and Khalid wants to help the earth and be an environmentalist. Maybe Peter will raise sheep like his family has always done. We all have so many interests. I still don't know what I'll be, but I think I have learned that I can be anything I want if I work hard and follow my dream. I also learned that it's fun to share my thoughts with my new friends and have found out that we are all thinking about similar things like world peace, the environment, and our futures.

Whatever we will be, we will be ourselves; unique and special in our own way. Just like Enole wrote about the master plan when the world was created, each of us is an individual, and together we make a beautiful painting. And like Maria, I also wonder about the huge world around us. From the Grand Canyon to the Himalayas, there are vast deserts, and overgrown jungles, and rain forests, and rivers that go for miles and miles. And there are so many animals: elephants, hippos, and zebras; kangaroos, koalas, and crocodiles; bears, birds, and butterflies; monkeys and llamas; sea otters and sheep; not to mention all the different kinds of fish! I tried to draw all the things I learned about from my new friends in one giant world map, so that when I look at it hanging on my wall, I can try to imagine what it's like to live in one country or another. What would it be like to eat the same foods and go to the same schools and pray the same way that my pen pals do? I think there is someone watching over us, but it doesn't matter what we call him (or her!). And it doesn't matter how or where we talk to him. It could be in a church, or a mission. We could go to a synagogue or face Mecca to pray five times a day. Even if you just go for a walk on the beach, you can appreciate and give thanks for the world we have and everything in it.

I'm really glad my mom told me about Samantha Smith. She was my inspiration. Without her, I might not have written to any pen pals or even made this scrapbook. And I've learned so much. The biggest thing is, no matter how different we are, we're all very similar. After all, we live on the same planet, drink the same water, and breathe the same air. And, like Michi, I think if we learn to respect and trust each other, we can all live together peacefully. So I guess I'd better get started. I'm going to try to do something nice for someone every day, even if it's for my brother. Maybe I'll help my him with his homework, or talk to a new kid in school who doesn't know anybody. And if it works like a boomerang like Peter says, or good karma like Deepa believes, then that's good, isn't it? And, like Michi meditating in her father's garden, I am going to spend some time in nature every day. If I can be peaceful within myself, I can be peaceful toward others.

my pen pals

Australia	Israel	Nigeria
Canada	Italy	Peru
China	Japan	Russia
France	Mexico	Saudi Arabia
Germany	Netherlands	Scotland
India		USA

get started today!

Now that my scrapbook is finished, I don't want my project to end. I think I'll start a club or something. I'll call it Pen Pal Kids Around the World. What do you think? To write to a pen pal, all you have to do is join. Fill out the form that came with this book and send it back to us. You'll get at least one name of a pen pal, a certificate of membership, and a neat T-shirt.

And if you want to make some fun craft projects, there is *My Pen Pal Workbook*. The workbook includes drawings and patterns for all the kids in the scrapbook, and instructions for coloring and cutting out the patterns to make decorations for your room, dolls, pillows, a quilt, T-shirt art—all kinds of things. You can work with crayons (for little kids), colored paper, wallpaper, or fabric. Let your imagination go wild. Mom helped me make a quilt. It was a lot of work, but worth it! I use it on my bed, and it reminds me of my new pen pal friends every day.

If you want to make your own pen pal scrapbook, you can get started right away. Even before I got letters from my pen pals, I went to the library to find information about each of the countries I wrote to. I like to draw, so I made drawings using pictures I found in the encyclopedia, magazines, and books about each country. But you can also cut out pictures from magazines. I also found some neat old postcards and stamps in a shop near my house in Carmel. Then I started asking my parents' friends where they had traveled and whether they had any souvenirs they wanted to contribute to my scrapbook (that's how I got most of the coins and bills). Then my mom got the idea for the quilt, and she wants to start making dolls too. And finally, when the letters started coming, my pen pals sent me pictures of themselves and their families, and other great stuff like the chopsticks from China, the handkerchief from Italy, and angels and dolls for my collections.

My summer project has lasted a lot longer than summer vacation. I just can't believe how much I have learned and how many new friends I have made. Now I need to write back to all my pen pals and send them things from the United States. I can't wait to see what they write back this time. I hope you have as much fun as I have had when you make your scrapbooks.

Love life and it will love you back!
Good Luck,

Jessica